96

UNLOCKING THE FAMILY DOOR

A Systemic Approach to the Understanding and Treatment of Anorexia Nervosa

UNLOCKING THE FAMILY DOOR

A Systemic Approach to the Understanding and Treatment of Anorexia Nervosa

By

Helm Stierlin
&
Gunthard Weber

BRUNNER/MAZEL *Publishers* • New York

Library of Congress Cataloging-in-Publication Data

Stierlin, Helm.
   Unlocking the family door : a systemic approach to the
understanding and treatment of anorexia nervosa / by Helm Stierlin &
Gunthard Weber.
      p.   cm.
   Translation from German.
   Bibliography: p.
   Includes index.
   ISBN 0-87630-541-9
   1. Anorexia nervosa—Patients—Family relationships. 2. Family
psychotherapy. I. Weber, Gunthard. II. Title.
[DNLM: 1. Anorexia Nervosa. 2. Family Therapy—methods. WM 175
S855u]
RC552.A5S79 1989
616.85'2—dc19
DNLM/DLC
for Library of Congress   88-26276
                                                               CIP

Published by
BRUNNER/MAZEL, INC.
19 Union Square
New York, New York 10003

MANUFACTURED IN THE UNITED STATES OF AMERICA

10 9 8 7 6 5 4 3 2 1

Contents

Preface

The title we have given this book is meant to emphasize one of the central features of the families here under study. It suggests that families have doors. Doors in houses are both a means of communication and a way of setting boundaries. They enable people both to be alone and to seek contact with others, to blend autonomy and togetherness. The relational climate within a family is partly regulated by the ideas the family has of the status of interpersonal doors and the use to be made of them. There is a difference between a family in which doors are considered superfluous and can thus be taken off their hinges for good and a family in which the door to every member's room has chains, bolts, and padlocks. There is a difference between doors with two handles and doors with a handle on one side only, and a difference between homes in which you have to knock before entering and homes where everyone has free right of access to everyone else. This book is about such differences.

Anorectic behavior can be viewed as an active attempt at self-cure that, again and again, confronts these girls with partitions, doors, and locks. With their hunger strike they are putting up walls, drawing dividing lines, or else establishing togetherness where there is a threat of separation. The tragic thing about this attempt is that it involves withdrawing into an interior (an interior as small as a pantry or a hermit's cell) and holding the door closed from the inside. The girls' own needs, the other members of the family, and the outside world are all to be kept at bay. It is an attempt to stage a necessary conflict, but the venue is one that precludes any progress. The family in its anxiety tries in vain to penetrate this interior and in the crippling stalemate that ensues it is frequently hard to distinguish those confined inside and those on the outside trying to get in. All are wards and wardens. A title such as Hilde Bruch's *The Golden Cage* (1978) implies confinement. We find it difficult to distinguish the victims from the perpetrators.

Preoccupation with the doors *within* a house means neglect of the significance of the door *to* a house. If the outside world is felt to be hostile and dangerous, then this door is probably kept locked and bolted. If the rule obtains that there is no return through that door, that one is either on the inside or the outside, then one will avoid or fear leaving the house at all. A teacher of ours once said that real independence means not slamming the door of one's parents' home behind one, but closing it softly and going back from time to time. This book is also about such different relational doors—about invitations and exclusions, penetration and isolation, door bells and alarm systems. It is also about the efforts made by family therapists not to barge their way in or use a battering ram to force open a door.

Many therapists think they know from the outset what entrances and exits exist for a family and when they should be used. We try, together with the families we treat, to look at a large number of different doors, fire-escapes, and trapdoors. Frequently we have family members invent invisible doors and try them out in our interviews to see what things are like on the other side. Therapists have no "right of access," no claims to a master key. Sometimes we may succeed in fashioning skeleton keys together with the family, and those lock-picking instruments may prove useful for the members of the family in expanding their potentials. We realize that families with anorectic members—and particularly these young women themselves—have a great range of potential skills at their disposal and we have frequently witnessed how they actually make use of them. Let us then open the first door and see where it leads.

Acknowledgments

This book could not have been written without the constant stimulation and encouragement given us by Fritz B. Simon, Gunther Schmidt, and Arnold Retzer. As members of our Heidelberg team they served also as cotherapists, observers, and discussants in many of the treatments surveyed in this book, as did Angelika Hahn and Bernd Schmid also. Maria Syska and Helene Michel were tireless in providing secretarial help. Karl Eugen Graf assisted in the statistical analysis, and Hans Hoffmann in the graphic presentation of the data. Andrew Jenkins translated most of the chapters from German into English. Ann Alhadeff, as editor, helped us inestimably with the final English version. We owe all of them our thanks. But most of all, we would like to thank our patients and their families for bearing with us and letting us learn so much from them.

Heidelberg, November 1988   *Helm Stierlin*
                                               Gunthard Weber

UNLOCKING THE FAMILY DOOR

A Systemic Approach to the
Understanding and Treatment
of Anorexia Nervosa

1

A Family with an Anorectic Daughter

Every family has a history all its own, a set of traditions unique to it. Also, every family has its own context, one in which relationships have developed and from which internal maps—the fundamental assumptions, the rules, and the values of the family members—have emerged and continue taking shape. But if we look more closely at families in which anorectic behavior manifests itself, we find that for all the differences they present, there are certain recurrences and similarities in the relational constellations, interactional patterns, and internal maps discernible within them.

While not losing sight of the differences, in this book we attempt to describe these recurrent phenomena in "anorexia families." It must be left to the reader to decide whether the factors that we feel we have identified coincide with his or her own experience of such cases and, if so, of what (potential) therapeutic value their identification may be. Naturally we will focus on problematic patterns and factors that favor the emergence of this particular disorder. At the same time, however, we will be careful from the outset to underline the positive forces and potentialities active or

1

inherent in these families: the high degree of concern and caring for one another, the marked sense of family cohesion, and the moral awareness and sensibility of the anorectic sufferers themselves.

It would not be a true reflection of our attitude toward the families we have treated if, after reading this book, they or others like them felt that they had been disparaged or stigmatized, held morally responsible for this disturbance that has appeared in their midst. On the one hand, we observe in the progress of events and the way relationships develop how each individual has become. On the other hand, we are at pains to give personal responsibility—whether actual or potential—its due. In the following chapters we describe typical constellations and processes. But that does not mean that we look upon them as immutable and inevitable. On the contrary, in the later section on therapy for such families, we hope to demonstrate how the scope for independent and responsible decisions can be extended and latent developmental potential activated and encouraged.

THE LANDMANN FAMILY

We begin by describing the case of one of the families we treated during the last 10 years. In this chapter we want to provide a capsule portrait of the family members and their relationships with each other, utilizing information we obtained in the course of 12 interviews, yet refraining, as much as possible, from interpreting the facts of the case. In Chapter 10 we will once more return to this family and then focus on their therapy.

The Genogram

The Landmann family is upper middle class and has six members. Mr. Landmann (age 50) is a senior-level civil servant; he is very precise and orderly, a "model citizen" who works very hard and attempts to solve problems sensibly and rationally and to preserve absolute integrity.

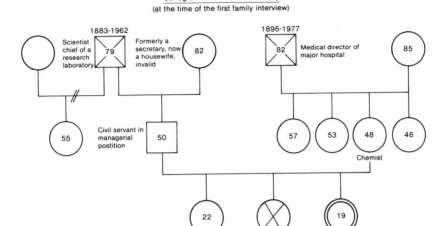

Genogram of the Landman family
(at the time of the first family interview)

Mrs. Landmann, the mother, is 48 years old and works part-time in a chemical laboratory. She appears somewhat careworn. She runs the large house single-handed so that she can be sure that everything is as it should be. Over and above this she is preoccupied to the point of self-denial with the welfare of all the other members of the family. As long as she is there, she says, her husband will not collapse under the burden of his duties. She tends to keep to herself any problems she may have and to retreat into her shell in difficult situations.

The older daughter, Jutta (age 22), left home four years previously and is an ambitious and successful student of art history in Cologne. She has a boyfriend but otherwise does not have many friendships. However, she does not consider herself to be lonely: "I was never the center of attention. I am my own center of attention and prefer to be independent." In conflict situations, she tends to "switch on the ice-box," (as she says). She intends neither to marry nor to have children. If she continues organizing her life as she has done so far, then by her own admission the most fitting motto for her general attitude would be: "The only

person you can trust all your life, the only one who's always
there, is yourself."

The 19-year-old Petra is the identified patient. She sees herself
as emotional in her reactions and having stay-at-home "wife-
and-mother" qualities. She feels she lacks singleness of purpose,
often having good intentions but being unable to summon up
the staying power to see them through.

The family also comprises the two grandmothers, who live in
separate apartments within the house. Mr. Landmann's 82-year-
old mother has been suffering for some time from loss of memory,
persecution mania, and pathological jealousy. She is described as
being in need of care. The maternal grandmother is 85 years old
and described as being in reasonably good health and possessing
"the ability to integrate."

THE PROBLEM

The family is referred to us by a doctor friend as being in crisis
and in urgent need of help. Petra has been suffering from anorexia
nervosa for some three years. Recently discharged from a psychosomatic clinic after an unsuccessful nine-month course of
treatment, she now weighs about 70 pounds (she is 5'7" tall). On
her return home it appears that the old quarrels about her eating
habits—particularly between herself and her father—have flared
up once again. These frequently follow an established pattern.
Her father thinks the problem can be solved by "energy and will
power." He tells Petra, with varying degrees of severity, to get
a grip on herself and eat more. The mother, on the other hand,
feels that Petra's behavior shows that she is sick; she tries to
protect her daughter and to convince her "in a friendly way"
that she must eat more. When Jutta is present, however, she
tends to adopt her husband's attitude.

RELATIONSHIPS WITHIN THE FAMILY

Although all the members of the family are greatly concerned
about not hurting each other and are thus reluctant to speak of

the differences that exist in the various relationship constellations, the following picture gradually emerges.

The Relationship Between the Parents and Their Daughters

Relationally, the mother is the nodal point within the family. All its members speak to her most. Petra sees here a kind of "pyramid" with everybody leaning for support on the mother, who then goes up into the next-floor apartment to consult with *her* mother. In the father's opinion, the mother is at present closest to their "problem child": "My wife invariably turns to the person who needs her most in a given situation." This statement implies that if one desires more intensive contact with the mother, then the best way to achieve this is to be a cause of concern. Confronted with this inference, Petra replies: "That's not the way I see it at all. I think Mommy has changed sides. Now that Jutta's left home she tends to take her part more." A certain rivalry between the two sisters becomes apparent. Petra seems to emphasize it more stirringly, often feeling neglected and left out. When the three women are together, Petra says, she is ignored like a small child while mother and Jutta discuss all kinds of plans. When the three of them are in the kitchen talking and Mrs. Landmann leaves the room for some reason, Jutta follows her immediately, leaving Petra on her own again.

As an example of this general tendency Petra describes how the idea of buying an apartment of their own for the family was discussed extensively with Jutta, whereas she herself only heard of it by chance. She says that this attitude is not one that stems to any real degree from her father, who has a great deal of work to do and is consequently away from home very often. In Petra's eyes he has always been closer to Jutta. The father himself says: "Jutta and I have more interests in common," adding that in earlier years Mrs. Landmann had been closer to Petra, who often helped her with the housework.

All members of the family agree about one general tendency: when two of them are together things are fine; as soon as a third member appears on the scene, tensions develop. And this seems inevitable as the third member cannot tolerate being excluded for long and the twosome cannot tolerate seeing the third member excluded.

The Relationship Between the Sisters

Petra and Jutta had, by their own admission, little interest in one another when they were girls. Both went their different ways and moved in different circles. Petra says to Jutta: "We only got on as long as you were the goddess and I was trying to be just like you and as long as I did everything you wanted. . . . I certainly don't see Jutta as the great academic who mustn't be distracted from her work. 'No, no, leave poor Jutta alone, she's got so much to do!' That's something I find pretty difficult to swallow. . . ." According to a violin teacher they had when they were young, there was a great deal of rivalry between them in the latency phase. If one of them had something, the other wanted it, too. As Jutta was more ambitious and hard-working, she always had better grades than her sister. The parents had held up Petra's goodness, gentleness, and helpfulness as an example to Jutta, and Jutta's achievements and intelligence as an example to Petra. Petra says: "There's a lot of envy on my part. If I were less envious I would have greater peace of mind." She says she has always envied Jutta for being slimmer and having finer facial features.

The Relationship Between the Parents

Mrs. Landmann tells us that she and her husband have very little time for one another. Having to look after their parents has meant that they have only ever had one real vacation together. Mr. Landmann says that it is a source of regret to him that his wife's concern for their parents has placed such restrictions on their married life.

The Landmanns met when they were 18 and 15 years old, respectively. When they married eight years later it was, we are told, a love match. Mrs. Landmann was not, however, received into her husband's family with any great welcome, the reason being the father's displeasure at his son marrying instead of working toward an academic career, and the mother's jealousy of Mrs. Landmann having a university education and going out to work.

Relationships with the Grandparents

The paternal grandmother has been living with the family ever since the death of her husband 18 years ago. The family moved into the house of Mrs. Landmann's parents when the latter started getting old. From the time their parents began to show signs of no longer being able to manage by themselves, both Mr. and Mrs. Landmann have looked after their parents intensively. Of the two granddaughters, Petra is described as having a more heartfelt relationship with the two grandmothers than Jutta, who only visits them "out of a sense of duty."

Changes in Family Relationships Preceding Petra's Anorectic Behavior

Mrs. Landmann poignantly summarizes the situation that provoked Petra's condition: "The day my father died, Jutta—in line with previous plans—moved to Cologne. That was when Petra stopped eating." Her father, she says, was the "linchpin" of the family. All of them had respected and loved him, and she herself had been particularly fond of him, greatly missing him after his death. In that period she had often turned to Jutta for support, either calling her on the phone or writing frequent letters.

The death of the grandfather and Jutta's simultaneous departure from home seem to have been difficult events to come to terms with for this extremely cohesive family, although all its members insist that both these separations had been entirely foreseeable for them.

Positive Changes Attributable to the Symptoms of Anorexia Nervosa

Before Jutta left home there had been an increase in tension within the family, particularly at mealtimes. Mr. Landmann had often exploded "like a volcano" while Mrs. Landmann had not spoken to anyone for days on end, also refusing to cook meals. Whereas the mother describes herself as not knowing what real anger is and Jutta says that negative feelings are completely foreign to her, according to Petra, "they show their aggression by indirect means," her mother refusing to speak and withdrawing into herself and Jutta giving vent to it via apparently harmless but nonetheless spiteful needling. Petra sees herself as more like her father in such situations, while at the same time fearing that if she reacts aggressively her parents will shut themselves off from her and she will then no longer have a home of her own. Hence her tendency at an early age to try to be the cheery "life and soul" of the family.

Petra's anorectic behavior is seen as causing the parents to have more contact with one another, the same being true of Jutta and Petra, who have come to know and like each other better. Concern for Petra has led to increased contact between her and her mother, while Mr. Landmann is said to have been considerably less "explosive" over the last three years. In general, there has been a major relaxation of overall tension. Petra now feels, however, that there is a danger of a "deathly hush" in the house. If she doesn't do the talking, nothing gets said at all. "But I don't see why I should go on baring my soul if the others all stay silent."

AT THE TIME OF PETRA'S BIRTH

A colleague observing a session from behind the one-way mirror drew our attention to a casual remark that we had failed to register. Looking at the videotape, we hear Petra say to her father: "Don't mention Gabile ["Gabile" is a diminutive form in German] whatever you do." Questioned about this comment at the next session, Petra says (to her father): ". . . and you said you weren't going to say anything about Gabile because you didn't know how mother might react and you didn't want her to start crying her eyes out. So you didn't mention it at all, although you think of it yourself every year on that particular day."

Gabi was a baby of the Landmanns who was born two months premature because of an inoculation given to the mother and who died on Jutta's first birthday. The baby died immediately after birth and was then taken away by the hospital staff, apparently by order of the physician who wanted to spare Mrs. Landmann any further pain. Only the mother ever saw the child. On the doctors' recommendation, Gabi was taken to the pathology lab after her death and was not buried. Mr. Landmann comments: "My wife is always distressed when April approaches. All of us think of it. My wife knows that I'm thinking of it but we don't talk about it. After all, you don't have to talk about everything. And we don't want it upsetting our children." We also learn that Petra had a doll she called Gabile. The mother says it is surely understandable that she didn't want to lose another child. When Petra was three months old she caught an extremely dangerous infection and the doctors only just managed to save her life. A colleague of Mr. Landmann lost two children from the same infection. In her first year of life, Petra was hospitalized twice because her parents had been worried about bouts of diarrhea. That was also the year in which Mrs. Landmann had an ectopic pregnancy.

Mr. Landmann is described as not having had much interest in the children when they were small and not being a "model father" in that respect. He had only shown an interest in them when they started to speak. Jutta had been the one with the eating problem at first; her mother felt that she often did not eat enough. Later on, however, the photos they had of her showed that she had been entirely normal physically. As a child Petra was, by her mother's description, uncomplicated, likable, and rather plump. As she often helped out in the house, she was called "our little housewife" by the others.

On the subject of death and grief we learn in one of the interviews that the deaths of the two grandfathers had been particularly traumatic because in both cases the family had had to decide on the discontinuation of life-preserving medical aid (heart-lung machine and cardiovascular medication).

THE PARENTS' FAMILIES

Mr. Landmann is the only child of his father's second marriage. Petra tells us: "The first wife ran away with an actor to live wild and free." The daughter from this marriage stayed with the father initially but then joined her mother when she remarried. We are told that Mr. Landmann's relationship with his stepsister later improved thanks to Jutta's mediation. This stepsister is Jutta's godmother and the person after whom she allegedly models her behavior. She has been engaged three times but has never married, preferring her independence. We are told that she finds men too demanding; now, after her mother's death, she lives quietly with only her dogs for company.

Mr. Landmann's mother is 15 years younger than his father and was originally his assistant. We are told that her motives for marrying him were probably not so much love as respect and admiration. The father is described as being considerably more compassionate than the mother, whom her son feels to have been cool and rejecting. He says that there was no great affection on his part for either of his parents but that this did not worry him at the time. He assumes that it was a disappointment to his father that he did not study classical languages and go on to obtain a doctorate. He sees his father's ambitious nature as having been passed on to Jutta and announces with obvious satisfaction that she would have been an ideal daughter for his father.

There is little to be learned from Mrs. Landmann about her family. She has a defensive attitude and describes the family relationships as exclusively harmonious, emphasizing again and again that there was nothing remotely representing jealousy, envy, rivalry, or preferential treatment. She does tell us, however, that her sister had asthma and for that reason was given greater attention by the mother. Although there were no physical manifestations of any kind in the family, relationships were affectionate. All four sisters went to university and got degrees.

Petra, who comes across as the one most likely to directly face up to the conflict evasion patterns that occur within the family, says that on a number of occasions her father has been on the point of abandoning her mother and going to live elsewhere. Both parents deny this vehemently.

Mr. Landmann represents above all the desire to uphold such values as orderliness, thrift, duty, and achievement at work. He makes a point of picking up the weekly paper at the store himself and of regularly going to collect the statements at the bank so as to be able to make sure that their money is used for really important things. When his daughters wear extravagantly fashionable clothing, he is irate ("Get out of my sight!"). The language he uses and his attitude toward life are those typical of a conscientious German civil servant.

Mrs. Landmann represents the ideals of self-sacrifice, family cohesion, being there for others, and self-denial. Mr. Landmann, by contrast, emphasizes that these have never been his ideals. The daughters agree that their father is the more pleasure-loving of the two. When we imply, at one stage in the interview, that the mother also has a right to look out for herself more, her reaction is one of annoyance: "I've not been put into this world just to look after *myself!*" We are told that she often leaves packages she has received unopened for days; and like her own mother she can be very generous to others but hardly ever indulges herself in any way. Jutta is seen as continuing this kind of asceticism through self-discipline and a generally austere attitude; Petra is seen as avoiding extravagance but at the same time suffering from chronic indecision ("Should I or shouldn't I?").

Self-control is an ideal shared by the whole family. The father is the one most likely to "let himself go" on occasion. For example, the parents take Petra to the theater after having dinner at home. After the performance they go to a restaurant. Mr. Landmann orders steak. His wife is offended at this: "Didn't you have enough at home, are you still hungry?" and then despondently: "In that case I'm going to have a plate of salad." Mr. Landmann tells the waiter he doesn't want steak after all. Petra is in two minds about all this but tries to mediate between the two. She finds her father egotistic but at the same time feels that if he really wants something he should see that he gets it. She sees her mother as determined not to make any demands and not to bother anybody; the mother has, for example, had thoughts of suicide but never talks about it. She has a great deal of empathy with all the others. Mother says to Petra: "Of course, I feel bad when you feel bad. . . . That's the way we've been for 30 years. Each one of us knows exactly where the others are. We belong together and share everything." Mr. Landmann has the following epitaph for his wife's lifestyle: "She was there for others, her life belonged to the others."

There is one "black sheep" in the family, an uncle of Mr. Landmann. The Landmanns look down on him. Mr. Landmann says: "He made all his mistakes three times over and that's what killed him in the end. He gambled, smoked, drank, and wrecked three marriages that way." Another relative, a sister of Mrs. Landmann, is also looked at rather askance. She likes to eat well, is divorced, and drives a big car.

The subject of sexuality can only be dealt with superficially as long as the parents are present. The climate within the family is certainly not favorably disposed to physical pleasure. Petra says of Jutta that "inside she's the snuggle-up kind but outwardly she's like an old maid," and that she could walk through a red-light district without being propositioned, keeping men at arm's length by the mere expression on her face. Of herself, Petra says that she is capable of physical affection and has always looked for someone to envelope her completely and do everything for her, but that "little bit between affection and sexuality" is difficult for her to cope with.

Now that we have introduced the reader to a family with an anorectic daughter, we would like to shift the focus of our inquiry away from the individuals concerned and onto the larger social context in which these individuals live and interact with others.

2

Social Aspects

Today we have come to distinguish a trio of eating disorders: compulsive refusal of food (anorexia nervosa), compulsive overeating (bulimia) and chronic overweight or obesity. Of these anorexia nervosa is the longest established as an illness. It was described for the first time in the mid-19th century.* Bulimia (also called bulimia nervosa, hyperexia nervosa, and bulimarexia) made its debut as a classified disorder in 1980, appearing for the first time in the *Diagnostic and Statistical Manual of Mental Disorders* (DSM-III) (American Psychiatric Association, 1980). Since 1985 efforts have been made, particularly in the United States, to have chronic obesity recognized as an illness in its own right. However, original plans to include it already in DSM-III-R (American Psychiatric Association, 1987) did not materialize.

These eating disorders are distinct from one another in a number of essential ways. We refer to anorexia when the patients (the vast majority being young girls or women) restrict their con-

---

* Gull (1873) in England and Lasègue (1873) in France published almost simultaneously quite comprehensive descriptions of the anorexia nervosa syndrome. Since then internists, pediatricians, and psychiatrists have rediscovered it on countless occasions and given it a multiplicity of different names. A good general overview on the historical development is provided by Thomae (1961, pp. 11–30). The development since then is outlined in Bruch (1985). A recent account of the evolution of the concept of anorexia nervosa is given by Al-Alami et al. (1987).

sumption of food to a point where they remain 15% below the weight normal for their age and height. Bulimia describes a condition with recurrent bouts of compulsive eating together with vomiting and/or the use of laxatives and/or strict dieting or fasting; the weight of the patient however remains normal (or slightly subnormal). Tables 1 and 2 provide the DSM-III-R diagnostic criteria for anorexia nervosa and bulimia nervosa. Overweight (obesity) occurs if normal weight is exceeded by at least 20%, thus probably increasing the likelihood of disorders such as high blood pressure, diabetes, heart attacks and so on.

There are links, transitions, and hybrid states between these three eating disorders. For example, many anorectics do not only reduce their intake of food, but also have bouts of compulsive eating, induce vomiting, and use laxatives. These are designated as bulimic forms of anorexia. Certain obese persons again may be termed incompetent bulimics (i.e., those who fail to master the art of self-induced vomiting and the use of laxatives and lapse into resignation about their weight).

If we assume that there are necessary—conscious or unconscious—control mechanisms for regulation of food intake, then these eating disorders may be regarded as disorders of such

Table 1
DSM-III-R Diagnostic Criteria for Anorexia Nervosa

A. Refusal to maintain body weight over a minimal normal weight for age and height, e.g., weight loss leading to maintenance of body weight 15% below that expected; or failure to make expected weight gain during period of growth, leading to body weight 15% below that expected.

B. Intense fear of gaining weight or becoming fat, even though underweight.

C. Disturbance in the way in which one's body weight, size, or shape is experienced, e.g., the person claims to "feel fat" even when emaciated, believes that one area of the body is "too fat" even when obviously underweight.

D. In females, absence of at least three consecutive menstrual cycles when otherwise expected to occur (primary or secondary amenorrhea). (A woman is considered to have amenorrhea if her periods occur only following hormone, e.g., estrogen, administration.)

* Reprinted with permission from *Diagnostic and Statistical Manual of Mental Disorders, Third Edition, Revised,* p. 67. Copyright 1987 American Psychiatric Association.

Table 2
DSM-III-R Diagnostic Criteria for Bulimia Nervosa

A. Recurrent episodes of binge eating (rapid consumption of a large amount of food in a discrete period of time).

B. A feeling of lack of control over eating behavior during the eating binges.

C. The person regularly engages in either self-induced vomiting, use of laxatives or diuretics, strict dieting or fasting, or vigorous exercise in order to prevent weight gain.

D. A minimum average of two binge eating episodes a week for at least three months.

E. Persistent overconcern with body shape and weight.

* Reprinted with permission from *Diagnostic and Statistical Manual of Mental Disorders, Third Edition, Revised*, pp. 68–69. Copyright 1987 American Psychiatric Association.

mechanisms. In anorexia they function too well. The victims decide not to eat, they become emaciated, and then they suffer various kinds of physical disorders (e.g., disorders of their hormone balance, electrolyte metabolism, and metabolic processes in the brain), not infrequently of a potentially fatal nature. In the case of bulimia these control mechanisms are effective—normal weight is maintained—but the patients experience themselves not as in control but as at the mercy of their eating compulsions. In obesity, all the control mechanisms seem to have failed. Hence here, too, there are feelings of powerlessness, shame, and resignation.

Thus, eating disorders confront us with fundamental (one might say, philosophical) questions. To what extent can I/should I exercise self-control or let myself go? What attitude should I adopt toward my body and its needs? What value do body and food have for me? To what extent am I guided in this evaluation by my own ideas and expectations, to what extent by those from other sources? In short, in what sense can I/must I be autonomous, both in my relationship to myself and to others?

Who is going to ask him- or herself these questions? When and how will they present themselves? The answer depends largely on the historical and social situation. We can safely say that the problem of control and autonomy with regard to food will only pose itself where food is available in abundance. There are no indications of anorexia or bulimia among the poor peoples of the

Third World. And in those nations (as well as in many parts of Eastern Europe), obesity is normally considered not a disorder but a status symbol. Only in affluent Western consumer societies are people called upon to exercise self-control and demonstrate autonomy in the face of a surfeit of available food.

However, Western societies are not only consumer societies, but also meritocracies, pluralistic in their makeup, and subject to ever swifter change. This aggravates the problems of self-control, autonomy, and identity for those living in these societies, exposed as they are to a vast array of contradictory requirements and expectations. This can be seen particularly clearly in the way body and food are presented and conceived as values (or the opposite). On the one hand, the media are full of advertisements for high-caloric foods; on the other hand, those same media preach the desirability of slimness, physical attractiveness, and fitness and the accompanying need for self-control, dieting, and restriction.

It is not surprising that it is women who are most strongly affected by these contradictions. On the one hand, modern industrial society provides them with more opportunities for self-realization than ever before (e.g., in jobs that have until now been a preserve of men). This brings with it the necessity for women to make more decisions, to maintain their identity in the face of the goals and expectations of a still largely male-dominated environment, and to assert themselves in a competitive context. On the other hand, women are exposed to the overt and covert expectations that they should be both maternal and womanly, caring and giving, and at the same time sexually desirable. They are thus placed in dilemmas which, as recently shown by Orbach (1978, 1984, 1986), make it understandable that an increasing number of them should embark on a hunger strike which is directed against both themselves and society as a whole. The same theme has been elaborated by other authors.* However, we

---

* Boskind-Lodahl, 1976, pp. 436–448; Vandereycken & Pierloot, 1983, pp. 543–549. An excellent description of the dilemmas faced by modern women that potentially contribute to eating disorders is also to be found in Wynne and Wynne (1987, pp. 60–76).

must bear in mind that while many women are confronted by these dilemmas, only a relatively small (albeit growing) percentage of them present clear-cut symptoms of anorexia or bulimia. Thus the question is what factors are necessary for the social elements mentioned above to actually lead to a concrete case of anorexia or bulimia?

This question turns our attention first of all to the individual context, that is, the world as he or she experiences it, the motivational dynamics and internal conflicts involved, along with his or her specific way of perceiving, internalizing, and dealing with the offers, models, constraints, and expectations presented by society and the contradictions between them. There now exists a vast range of literature, summarized by Bruch (1973, 1978) and Orbach (1986) on the problem of anorexia as seen from this vantage point, including a number of accounts by anorexia victims themselves (e.g., MacLeod, 1981).

But the same question also turns our attention to the family context. Individuals are decisively marked and socialized by their family (occasionally by family substitutes). Whatever society has to offer in the way of values, expectations, models, and contradictions will be conveyed via the family, admittedly in a filtered and modified form. In other words, every single family appears as a scenario in which the internal maps, the self-esteem, the behavioral maxims, and the expectations, rights and duties of the individual members are internalized, perpetuated, or modified in a variety of ways.

It is our opinion that eating disorders (in this book we are focusing on anorexia nervosa) can only be properly understood and, in most cases, effectively treated if we include this scenario in our considerations. We further believe that these disorders manifest themselves in particular kinds of families (the Landmann family is an example) which differ significantly from other families (disordered or not). A framework within which we can work to grasp the essential features of these families who have an anorectic member is provided by the concept of *related individuation*.

3

Related Individuation

The features characterizing anorectic families and distinguishing them from other families can best be seen in a perspective that takes into account the changes and developments that will necessarily take place at certain stages in a family's ongoing history. In other words, a family can be regarded as a system which, paradoxical as it may seem, has to keep on changing in order to survive as a system. The changes that occur at certain points result from the various requirements inherent in the progress of the life cycles of the individual members and the family as a whole. The children grow up and leave home; the parents, left to themselves, once again have to reorganize their lives, perhaps assuming greater responsibility for their own aging parents, and so on. Other factors causing changes are such things as illness, moving to another town, the father losing his job, political and social upheavals, and other unforeseen events. We can say that the degree to which a family can be described as functional—or, if one prefers, healthy—stands in direct relation to the degree of success with which its members come to terms with such foreseeable and unforeseeable changes by reshaping their relationships, readjusting, and undergoing change themselves.

However, not all change is necessarily synonymous with development. We reserve use of the term "development" for cases in which the members of a family show evidence of a continuing process of individuation. By individuation we mean basically the following:

1. Being able and willing to draw internal and external boundaries, distinguishing clearly between *my* perceptions, *my* desires, *my* fantasies, *my* rights, and *my* duties (particularly those related to *my* body and its needs) and the perceptions, desires, fantasies, rights, and duties of others.
2. Being able and willing to define and successfully pursue aims and objectives of one's own which differ from those declared desirable by the environment.
3. Being able and willing to accept a broad range of contradictory and sometimes painful aspects of one's self and to hold up under the tension produced by such ambivalence.
4. Being able and willing to assume the responsibility for one's own behavior. (This is closely connected to #3.)

Individuation in this sense is typically accompanied by a feeling of personal freedom and autonomy. But this particular kind of autonomy includes the awareness of one's own dependence—on one's body, for example, and on the human and nonhuman environment—in the same way as a bird soaring up into the air is an apt symbol for freedom but at the same time remains dependent on the currents of air that keep it airborn.

Yet we can only speak of development in a family if individuation also means that the members do not only become more independent but at the same time shape their relationships—to persons both inside and outside the family—in new and usually more complex ways. Thus development means that there is progress to ever new levels of individuation *and* relatedness. Or, to put it another way, development means progress in *related individuation* (Karpel, 1976; Simon, 1988; Stierlin, 1978, 1983; Stierlin et al. 1980).

Naturally, this requirement—reaching ever new levels of related individuation—is one that mainly applies to Western industrial societies. And within them it applies particularly to children and adolescents attaining greater independence as they grow up and dissociate themselves (to a greater or lesser degree) from the family in order to establish relationships of their own and develop new forms of "partnership" with people outside their family of origin. It applies especially to the group of anorectics we are concerned with here. But in the last resort it also applies to all members of a family system, parents as well as children. Hence we will be talking about various stages of family-wide coindividuation and coevolution. However, successful coindividuation and coevolution make different demands on parents and children. If we look at those made on the parents we can say that for a child to individuate successfully his or her parents (particularly the mother) will first of all have to maintain a close relationship, attuned to the needs of the still highly dependent child and creating an atmosphere of stability and protection. Also, the parents will have to reduce the complexity of the world for the child, as long as this is necessary, by communicating to him or her clear and consistent rules, expectations, and values. At the same time, however, they must allow the child to delineate his or her own identity to an increasing degree and, if need be, to individuate *against* them, that is, by distinguishing his or her own desires, values, and notions from those of the parents and, if necessary, standing up for them in the face of parental opposition.

In other words, both parents and children must create a basis upon which the unavoidable conflicts that will occur can be explicitly seen as such and also worked out and settled. This means that the parties to the relationship must have a chance to formulate their different aims, interests, viewpoints, and values and to realize them as far as possible. But such differences in aims, interests, viewpoints, and values must not be allowed to lead to a discontinuation of dialogue within the family, either as a result of violent conflict or of a disintegration of the relationship. It seems fair to say that if this dialogue is to be successful, then the parties to it—here, parents and their children—must always be able to reestablish a fundamental consensus and reach agreement on what, for both sides, is a valid and workable kind of social and relational reality (Bateson, 1972, 1979; Stierlin, 1977, 1981a; Wirsching & Stierlin, 1982).

As we saw earlier, this relational reality stems entirely from the parents when a child is newborn or very young. But as the child grows up and individuates, there is an increasing necessity for this relational reality to be negotiated *between* parents and child. The extent to which this is successful will then have a direct influence on the extent to which conflicts and the various stages of separation can be faced and dealt with satisfactorily. If the partners in the relationship manage to negotiate and adhere to a form of relational reality acceptable to all involved, then we can safely expect conflict and gradual separation to be a loving battle, an amicable contest, a collaborative choreography of holding and letting go. But this kind of loving battle can only be said to exist if the desire for and the right to self-assertion are combined with the willingness and the ability to empathize with the viewpoint and the interests of one's partner(s) and to display a tendency toward compromise and flexibility. It is asking a lot of today's parents to make such a loving battle possible. It requires a blend of constancy, on the one hand, and flexibility and adaptability, on the other, a blend which itself needs to be carefully geared to the individual child's stage of development. It can involve establishing hard-and-fast rules for a 10-year-old which say that he has to be home at 8 o'clock at the latest and at the same time negotiating a modus vivendi for a 16-year-old which grants him greater freedom, while at the same time giving him greater responsibility for his own actions.

Experience with family therapy shows that finding a consensus or negotiating a workable form of relational reality, which is at one and the same time a prerequisite, expression, and consequence of successful progress in related individuation, is liable to fail in the context of certain scenarios. One of these—and here we arrive at our central thesis—is the kind presented by families with anorectic members.

4

The Families of Anorectics

By way of introduction to these families, we delineate below the ideal type of a family with an anorectic member. An ideal type (according to Max Weber [1913], who coined the term) is an artificial construct, a design that allows us to orient ourselves among the confusing array of interrelated social processes and systems and to proceed from there to comparative study. Such an ideal type may still serve its purpose perfectly well even if there is no actual case in reality (or what we consider reality) that matches it entirely. The Landmann family (described in Chapter 1) certainly does not match it in all aspects. The word "construct" (used above) points to the share that we as authors of this book have in "constructing" the ideal type we are about to describe. As family researchers and therapists, we are made aware again and again how much we ourselves, via our experience, perception, and evaluation of what we take to be essential and inessential factors, are constituent elements of the resultant image of a given family.

Both despite and because of our share in the design, our picture of the anorectic's family is a complex one. Like a telescope that concentrates on certain areas to the exclusion of others, depending on how it is placed or adjusted and the power of the lenses one uses, so in the following we use different angles and "adjustments" to try and provide a valid picture of the phenomenon we are examining.

We shall at first use a lens with a wider range of observation and so set our sights on the extended family, that is, the grandparents of the identified patient, and in some cases even the great-grandparents. In other words we have chosen a multigenerational perspective (Boszormenyi-Nagy & Spark, 1973; Boszormenyi-Nagy & Krasner, 1986; Sperling et al., 1982). We feel that this kind of perspective points up best what our experience has shown us to be typical of families with anorectics, that is, particularly strong and characteristic *binding* across a number of generations.

We have given fairly detailed descriptions elsewhere of various kinds or modes of binding (Stierlin, 1981b). Here suffice it to state that an example of binding, in our sense of the word, always materializes when certain feelings, basic assumptions, or values prevail among the relational partners (or they at least feel they should prevail) and then result in certain specific behavioral patterns. These patterns, in turn, affect the feelings, assumptions, and values from which they arose. We are dealing with interreacting elements within complex cause-and-effect mechanisms involving circular or recursive processes. These elements are difficult to describe in isolation. But if we are to deal with them at all, we must try to distinguish them from one another. We turn our attention first to the *basic assumptions* shared by the members of the family of origin.

These manifest themselves as an internalized code of behavior built up around such (implied) tenets as "giving is better than receiving," "self-denial makes you a finer person," "my own needs and desires are not so important as those of others," "I only feel OK if the others are feeling OK," "we are a band of people forged together by destiny; none of us must be left by the wayside."

This dedication to family cohesion, self-sacrifice, and denial soon manifests itself as a binding dynamic that is sure to interfere seriously with progress toward individuation and family-wide coindividuation and coevolution.

A frequent accompaniment to self-sacrifice, which emphasizes the welfare of the family as a whole and denies the gratification of personal needs and desires, is a marked impulse control, represented most clearly in the case of the Landmanns by the mother. The family commandment is: "You must control yourself, you must not let yourself go." This applies to the temptations of both food and sexuality. And self-control also means keeping one's feelings in check at all times, presenting a friendly and controlled outward appearance and, in particular, suppressing hostile and "bad" (i.e., hurtful, offensive, disparaging, irate, or envious) feelings or attitudes. For the most part, it is best not to make oneself conspicuous in any way but rather, to make a point of living up to the expectations of others, not only parents, grandparents and relatives but also neighbors and society in general. This usually means adjusting to the norms upheld by the environment, being conventional, and being willing to react with feelings of profound guilt and shame if one deviates from those norms.

Frequently this kind of preoccupation with social adjustment also involves the internalization of *achievement ideals*, both those arriving from legacies and delegations (Stierlin, 1978, 1981b) within the family and those stemming from the expectations and values of society (family and society ideals are often mutually supportive to the point of becoming indistinguishable). Hence, the members of these families are often hard-working, ambitious, and highly respected citizens over a number of generations.

Here we need to mention a further feature typical of such families, their *sense of justice*. In the parents this often takes the form of a self-imposed injunction to love and treat all their children alike. No child must be preferred, no child short-changed, emotionally or otherwise. In one of the families we encountered, this internalized fairness injunction meant that whenever there was an extra-special dessert at lunchtime, a certain ritual was performed: all the children had to stand in a line against the wall, turn their eyes away from the dessert, and decide "blind" who got which portion. This concern with fairness, together with the preoccupation with family cohesion described above, militates against all (open) alliances or coalitions within the family. As everyone has equal rights to love and acceptance, nobody needs to set him/herself apart from the family as a whole or one of its subgroups.

This fairness injunction is a particularly clear demonstration of the degree to which certain kinds of contradiction, conflict, and dilemma are programmed to appear in these families. However desirable—indeed imperative—family-wide justice may seem to its members, however completely they may have internalized these requirements, certain preferences or unfairnesses (temporary or permanent) are bound to occur in the course of ongoing family life. These then have to be negated or phased out of the overall family awareness and dialogue. This, in turn, means that the members of the family, and the children in particular, are exposed to contradictory messages. The parents' official party line and their actual behavior (or the feelings they display in certain situations) fail to add up. One recovered anorectic put it this way: "My mother was always saying that it was equal rights and fair shares for everyone and no exceptions. But day in, day out I could see that the twins (three years older) were given more attention and affection both within the family and outside. But she still insists that this was not the case. I ended up by resigning myself to the fact that that's the way things were. But it annoys me to see her still sticking to the same old line."

Thus the extreme concept of fairness in many of these families emerges as a further element in a dynamic that reinforces binding and hampers individuation, if it does not prevent it altogether. As we saw in the last chapter, individuation means the perception, toleration, and acceptance of differences and separateness, as well as of ambivalence. A family creed that so insistently demands and idealizes family cohesion, family harmony, and equal treatment for all by all will maintain a vicelike grip on its members and block any kind of movement toward separation or individuation.

Individuation has *separation* implicit in it. Emotionally, however, "separation" as used in everyday language is something more incisive and profound than individuation. The word separation evokes existential experiences that have indeed had a very marked influence on the attitudes, relational climate, and expectations of many of the anorectic families we have come across.

Upon closer scrutiny these families proved to have an unusually high incidence of early separations and sudden, disastrous losses that appeared to spread like shock waves over the following generations without ever subsiding entirely. When she was a child, one mother saw her small brother, whom she was supposed to be looking after, fall to his death. In other cases, parents or important close relatives died in unexplained circumstances which have lived on in the memory of the family members and are either explicitly recalled at regular intervals or else consciously hushed up and repressed. In her account of her own life, MacLeod (1981) also points to the significance of separations and losses in her family. In many cases, the circumstances of these separations and losses bring into question whether different behavior or greater vigilance might not have prevented these deaths. Thus the (finally unanswerable) question of the cause of death is always bound up with the (also finally unanswerable) question of who was to blame. The Greek word *aitia*, which is the root of the term "etiology," means both cause *and* guilt and serves to remind us what a long tradition of thought and language use it is that prompts us to connect the question of causation with that of guilt or blame.

In many of the families we have seen there are strikingly frequent references to cases of tragic loss, death, uprooting, and separation experienced by the parents or grandparents of our patients during World War II: for example, when fleeing before the advance of the Russian troops toward the end of the war. These experiences have gone echoing down through the generations to the present.

Thus the ubiquity of loss and separation anxieties is a further factor in the "bound-upness" of these families, a further motivation for their members to stick together at all costs, to cling to

one another, and at the same time to rely on each other unquestioningly and hence maintain hope of survival in a dangerously unpredictable world. This, in turn, means that fears of
separation and loss are transformed into concern or, if one prefers,
loving care and an increased feeling of responsibility for the
others. This feeling of concern and responsibility often tends to
center on the physical well-being of the others. The mothers of
our anorectic patients seemed particularly prone to such concern,
constantly asking themselves anxiously whether they were sufficiently involved with the child, guarding over her health, keeping
others away from her, and above all giving her enough to eat.

THE MARRIAGES OF PARENTS OF ANORECTICS

The parents of anorectic girls are characterized by the attitudes,
assumptions, and values described earlier. Thus they represent
models that they themselves had emulated in their own parents.

Such models communicate themselves above all in processes
that we have described elsewhere as delegation (Stierlin, 1981b).
They grow from a strong bond of loyalty, which makes children
sensitive to the hopes, desires, and expectations conveyed to them
overtly or covertly by the parents. These expectations may be
beyond the capacity of the child; they may force her into a very
one-sided development and may sooner or later involve her in
a variety of conflicts and problems. Thus we found frequently
that mothers in our sample would, on the one hand, anxiously
hover over the anorectic daughter, enlist her as a source of
concerns, as it were, and, on the other hand, treat her as an
adult (i.e., parentified) confidante and ally in a coalition directed
against the father.

The degree to which children are exposed to the pressure of
such parental delegation and the degree to which they give in
to it depend on a number of factors that we cannot go into more
closely here due to space limitations. Even in a very strongly
bound-up family, children may still manage to find a niche for
themselves in which they can develop with a comparatively high
degree of latitude (i.e., not weighed down by parental expectations)
and which at the same time gives them the opportunity of earning

the approval of the parents later on. Such children find it easier to free themselves from the grip of the family and make progress toward all-around individuation than those who are more accepting of binding delegation and/or are considered to be more suitable and receptive in this respect.

In our study, the parents of anorectics often turned out to be the children in their own families who were most willing to fulfill the expectations of their parents and were thus most strongly influenced by their parents' attitudes and value judgments. This means that they are the children most likely to look after their parents when these later become old and frail and most likely to take them into their homes, thus demonstrating that they are the ones to have most completely internalized the family creed of self-sacrifice, self-control, family cohesion, and fair treatment for all members. In a straight comparison, as illustrated in the case of the Landmanns, this usually applies even more to the mother than to the father. This binding to their own parents also makes it easier to comprehend something that has repeatedly struck us in our clinical work, that these parents often marry relatively late and in doing so try to choose a certain kind of partner.

To the extent that these parents have accepted and adopted the family creed, particularly about not letting oneself go and controlling oneself and one's passions, they may also be expected to be repelled and/or disappointed sooner or later by romantically inclined partners, that is, those likely to be uninhibited, unconventional, and sexually demanding. In other words they find such partners incompatible, experiencing them as frivolous and unreliable. After such disappointments, they tend to go for (frequently quite late in life) someone who can guarantee them orderliness, reliability, and social security. In a mixture of resignation and relief they decide in favor of a "marriage of convenience," in which mutual caring, understanding, and harmony are more important than "love." Marital sex loses significance. The partners find it more important to be good parents to their children and good children to their own parents than good lovers for one another. Hence they take their parental duties very seriously. Where the fulfillment of these duties is concerned, we tend to find traditional role sharing. The mother is responsible for running the home and looking after the children, the father is the bread-winner and generally responsible for the social status and financial security of the family.

The apparent absence of strong passions, the binding forces already described, and the traditional distribution of roles frequently combine, despite the tensions below the surface, to make such marriages sturdier and longer-lived than many more "modern" (quasi-)marital relationships in which—not least because of the desire for greater self-assertion and emancipation evidenced by many women today—there are more open conflicts, more rocky patches, more ups and downs, and in the final analysis, more separations. Indeed, we and other researchers (e.g., Minuchin, Rosman, & Baker, 1978) have continually been struck by the stability of the marriages of the parents of anorectics (something that apparently does not apply to the same degree to the parents of bulimic daughters).

This stability in the marriages of anorectics' parents is often achieved at the expense of a certain restrictedness and rigidity. These marriages have difficulties in meeting the challenges for change and development, the crucial reason being the attitudes and behavior patterns already described.

In our fast-moving age, the ability to develop requires partners to constantly redefine their own individual identities vis-à-vis each other, to accept conflict, to withstand disharmony and the tensions born of ambivalence, and at the same time to remain in constructive communication with one another. And this development is made extremely difficult, if not impossible, by marital relationships governed by the motto that one must not let oneself go, must preserve harmony, must respect conventions, and must stick together at any price.

THE IMAGE OF A BOUND-UP FAMILY—
FIRST CONCLUSIONS

Now that we have looked at the grandparents and the parents of anorectic girls, it is time to turn to the patients themselves within the context of the family. First of all, however, we wish to pause to reaffirm a number of things about that family context, most of which derive directly from what we have said so far.

To start with, we return to what is probably the most general feature, the characteristically high degree of *binding* (both within the immediate family and over a number of generations). This "bound-upness" finds expression in almost all structures and processes to be observed in the family. Inwardly, it manifests itself in a tendency toward fusion, the dismantling or blurring of boundaries between individuals and generations, and a seismographic sensitivity toward the mental and emotional processes of the others. Outwardly, this kind of binding leads to impermeability, building walls against impulses, information, and novelties coming in from the outside world, and representing a potential danger to the cohesion and stability of the family. In other words, there is rejection of all that could trigger family-wide coindividuation and coevolution.

Such a family reminds us of a house in which all the rooms are interconnected and all the doors are open. Frequently, this is quite literally the case: It is always possible for any member of the family to enter another's room—his or her private domain—without knocking. Often even the parents' bedroom will be left open and not have a lock on the door. One family complained that a new house they had moved into had not had any inside structural improvements. At the same time, however, the house was from the very beginning double-locked and sealed against possible intruders.

Minuchin, a pioneer in the therapy and study of families of anorectics, was the first to describe essential features of such binding and "bound-upness" in these families. Their main structural characteristics, as described by Minuchin and his co-workers, are enmeshment (above all the tendency for boundaries between family members and generations to blur), overprotectiveness, rigidity, and conflict avoidance (Minuchin, Rosman, and Baker, 1978, Rosman et al., 1977). Also, Minuchin and his co-workers were among the first to point to the significance of the "unclosed doors" (Aponte & Hoffmann, 1973).

Another family typology covering central features of anorectics' families is that of Beavers (1977, 1981; Beavers & Voeller, 1983). His typology is based on the assessment of competence, adaptability, and the direction in which families develop. With this model, Beavers has the families with anorectic members located among the borderline centripetal families. Beavers adopted the term "centripetal" from Stierlin, who later designated centripetal families as "binding families" (Stierlin, 1981b; Stierlin et al. 1973). Thus, in the following, we use the latter term.

According to Kelsey-Smith and Beavers (1981), centripetal families present the following characteristics:

1. They have rigid outer boundaries.
2. There is a restriction of attempts toward autonomy and separation, the major significance being attributed to cohesion.
3. Members project their desires for satisfaction of emotionally significant needs onto the family; the outside world is looked upon as a threat.
4. Conflicts are avoided.
5. The parental coalition is largely effective, parental relations correspond to a domination/submission pattern.
6. Words have a high status.
7. Families come for therapy but tend to delegate their problems to the therapists.

Apart from the statements on parental coalition and the importance of words, these characteristics are, in our view, also typical of many anorectic families.

The characteristics listed may be understood as the consequence and/or expression of the family creed to be observed in the families of origin and in the parents and the relational patterns deriving from that creed. It is, however, also possible to see these characteristics as mutually conducive factors in a binding relational scenario. Thus overprotectiveness, for example, can be seen both as an expression and a consequence of a high degree of binding. We can say that it stems from binding and creates more binding. This, in turn, means that the boundaries between individuals and subsystems within the family—particularly the subsystems of the different generations—will become increasingly blurred, with a tendency for fusion to predominate. This is matched by the whole family's concern to maintain harmony and the general avoidance of, and ban on, conflict. But to the degree that conflicts and differences are suppressed and left inexplicit, pent-up aggression will begin to make itself felt behind the harmonious exterior. This aggression, as seen by Petra Landmann, takes indirect channels. Hence it triggers a family-wide reaction formation—in other words, even greater efforts toward harmony, even more protectiveness. This, in turn, means that the system has to close itself off even more completely from the threat of change (perhaps more accurately, from any information that might spell change). Hence, there is greater cohesion, greater binding, greater enmeshment, greater rigidity, and so on.

Another characteristic of these families, probably first described by Minuchin, is the absence of a clearly defined hierarchy and leadership structure, both despite and because of the stability that characterizes them and the more or less traditional and complementary way in which the parents divide their roles. In crisis situations (meaning situations in which changes seem to be about to happen), there is a leadership vacuum. The parents paralyze and sabotage each other, particularly where questions of the children's upbringing are involved. As soon as one parent makes demands on a child, the other moves directly or indirectly to his/ her defense, accusing the other parent of too much strictness or unfairness, insisting that the child is incapable of carrying out what has been asked of him/her, starting to cry, and so forth (Minuchin et al., 1978, Selvini Palazzoli, 1974). Typically—and this is true in the Landmanns' case—one parent sees the child in question as weak and/or sick, the other as disobedient or insufficiently motivated. These differences may go so far as to disrupt the family harmony which is otherwise always under control.

Where power relations are ill-defined and leadership structures nonexistent, there is a danger that power struggles will be fought out "underground," with the result that the leadership vacuum increases even further. These underground battles are also governed by rules, rules compatible with the family values and regulations already mentioned. The blanket "commandment of selflessness" will inevitably lead to rivalry over who gives more, sacrifices more, controls him/herself best, suppresses his/her own needs most effectively, and so on. Within such rivalry, any attempts at autonomy and self-realization will be branded as self-centeredness and then blocked in a process of reciprocal exacerbation. Anyone who takes a little more for him/herself than the others, and perhaps is a little more capable of pleasure and enjoyment than they are, is accused of letting him/herself go and taking the easy way out. Self-denial, by contrast, is a way of gaining prestige within the family.

In such a constellation, power will be gained by the member of the family who gives most, sacrifices most, and satisfies his or her own personal needs least. It is a kind of power that enables this morally superior member of the family (both in his/her own eyes and those of the others) to most effectively operate the guilt lever. The scene is thus set for a matyrdom contest, a competition in self-sacrifice. Our understanding of these dynamics in families of anorectics has been most notably enhanced by Selvini Palazzoli and her Milanese colleagues (Selvini Palazzoli, 1988, pp. 143–224; Selvini Palazzoli et al., 1978).

Now, where togetherness, loyalty, cohesion, and self-sacrifice are idealized and practiced to the extent found in these families, their opposites—disengagement, escape, betrayal, and self-centeredness—are bound to be present as both highly tempting and deeply feared phenomena. In fact, as far as these families are concerned, betrayal and escape are just as much universal existential realities as is the martyr game.

These realities manifest themselves in an area to which family therapists were quick to turn their attention: the formation of coalitions within the family. Even in clinically unremarkable families developing (more or less) normally, it is usual for individual members or subsystems to gravitate toward one another. Typical examples are siblings feeling a mutual attraction and having the same friends and the same interests, children who are the father's, mother's, or grandmother's "favorite," and so on. It is often hard to say whether this is more a case of special affinity or of alliances and coalitions. In any event, we must reserve the term "problematic (or pathological) coalition" for cases where such alliances involve irreparable schisms within the family or in other ways prevent family-wide coindividuation and coevolution from developing as it should. This is particularly the case when a child joins with an adult *against* another adult (i.e., parent or grandparent) and more especially when this alliance remains covert (Haley, 1967; Minuchin & Fishman, 1981).

What we have said about the belief prevalent in families with anorectics will have made it obvious that coalitions are going to be prohibited. These could, after all, be proof that not everyone is treated and loved equally by all the others. And yet here, too, like in any other family, there will be instances of particular affinities between individual members and hence divisions, preferences, and favoritism. These are, however, banished to and have to remain below the surface. But, as implied by what we have described so far, such covert alliances are only too readily interpreted—by both the allies and those excluded from their pact—as betrayal, deception, and a disregard of the family creed.

There is a further aspect of these families that will later prove significant: the fact that over the generations the family creed, with its demand for and idealization of giving, self-sacrifice, and selflessness, often manifests itself in an exaggerated or accentuated form in individual members. This can be observed especially in the mothers' families. In many of the families we have studied, the great-grandmother was (already) a particularly striking example of giving and self-sacrifice. The grandmother then went one step further, representing a saintly figure, who was always patient and always ready to help others. The mother took the same line, restricting herself even more than her mother and outdoing her in terms of self-sacrifice and altruism. Finally, the anorectic daughter appears as an even more rigorous champion of the family creed, taking it to absurd lengths. On the one hand she is even less self-indulgent, castigates and torments herself by means of a radical and consistent refusal to eat in a manner which puts all her predecessors to shame. At the same time she is interminably and tirelessly concerned with the psychological and, above all, physical welfare of the other family members, very often buying and cooking the meals for them with the greatest devotion and care. White (1983) has emphasized this "cumulative multigenerational dynamic," a phenomenon previously observed in Germany by Sperling and Massing (1970, 1972).

We thus have a transgenerational chain of escalating and internalized demands with regard to self-sacrifice. For the links in this chain a further significant consequence is discernible. A person who constantly practices self-sacrifice and constantly gives more than he or she receives is, by the same token, entitled to a reward (Boszormenyi-Nagy & Spark, 1973), which, as things stand, can best be claimed from the members of following generations, that is, the person's own children. Hence the subliminal message being conveyed to the child beneath the sacrifices of the mother is: "Look, I've given *my* mother, *my* parents so much, now it is up to *you* to repay me for this." And the more the child turns into an obedient and bound-up delegate of her mother, the more she attempts to satisfy the mother's (usually implicit) claims. This is sure to lead to dilemmas that only reveal their full virulence when the family is finally confronted with a case of anorexia nervosa in its midst.

THE CHILDHOOD OF THOSE WHO BECOME ANORECTICS*

In retrospect, children who later become anorectic frequently appear particularly parent-bound. But if we try to piece together

---

* We, the two authors, had some difficulty in reaching a consensus on the usefulness of the following paragraphs. One of us, seeing himself as an eager inventor (or co-inventor) of realities, was rather skeptical as to the value of speculations about how past events could possibly be linked to presently existing symptoms. He thought this was a domain more for the writers of novels than for therapists. Therapists, he felt, should be cautious not to insinuate that people are or are not okay. We regress too easily, he argued, "to

a more accurate collage of their childhood from accounts given by the girls themselves, their brothers and sisters, parents and grandparents, the picture becomes more complicated. Often the child's birth itself was surrounded by anxiety. The mother was particularly nervous during pregnancy and this nervousness was not without reason, as we discussed earlier, namely, the memory of sudden deaths, losses, and catastrophes as a result of (assumed) parental negligence. The Landmann family (described in Chapter 1) also suffered a loss of this kind: baby Gabi, prematurely born after an inoculation given to the mother, died on Jutta's first birthday. (It is by no means untypical for there to have been no mention of this death and for the anxiety, shock, and grief of the parents and the mother, in particular, not to have been shared, but remaining present for that very reason in the minds of the family members.)

Thus this child activates the mother's anxiety that something awful will happen if she does not take enough care as the child's mother. She sees the child as a challenge to her maternal capacities, someone to whom she must be as giving, loving, and protective as possible. Thus she frequently appears to be particularly preoccupied with the child—indeed, to love her more than the others (insofar as this can be reconciled with the family's equality ethic). But on a closer look we may find that this appearance is deceptive. It is not surprising that the mother frequently has unusually ambivalent feelings about this particular child. This first of all takes the form of an anxiously caring and protective attitude, a tendency to spoil and pamper the child, to fend off all possible dangers from her, and to make sure she has enough to eat. The motto seems to be: "I show you my love by giving you good things to eat and you show yours by eating well."

In a number of cases the parents have wanted a boy and, although this has never been mentioned or discussed within the family, they have been bitterly disappointed at the arrival of a

---

old habits of constructing simplistic and unidirectional cause-effect chains with a potential for generating guilt and defensiveness."

However, the other author believed it was legitimate and useful to share with the readers the following considerations. As an advocate of related individuation he professed his trust in their autonomous ability to judge things for themselves.

baby girl. Once the baby is born, the mother must realize that she will not be rewarded, given to, or liberated, but will be stuck with another burden, that is, a demanding child.

However, this is not a disappointment that she can admit to, as that would be too much at odds with her and the family's creed. The disappointment has to be split off or negated; but this will not prevent it finding expression in the mother's behavior. Through her actions she shows her ambivalent wishes to get rid of or reject her child. Nonverbally she communicates the fact that she would be far better off if she did not have the child or at least if the child were not such a burden. These wishes are not lost upon the child. The more sensitively attuned she is to her mother, the more likely she is to register her mother's understandable ambivalence toward herself. She will ask herself whether she is really loved and cherished for her own sake, without "ifs" and "buts." And this question will be with her throughout her childhood, without her ever finding a definite answer. A clear statement, after all, might mean having to accept the ambivalence and rejection desires of the mother, that is, realizing that she is not unquestioningly loved. So both the girl and the mother have a stake in keeping the answer in the dark. But as long as this existential question is neither clearly framed nor definitively answered, the ground is being prepared for a drama that will only later—when the anorexia nervosa manifests itself—reveal itself to its full extent.

We may then say that the form of binding we encounter in anorectics' families is almost invariably compounded by tremendous ambivalence and desires to reject, get rid of, and escape, along with feelings of anxiety and guilt. While the mother tries to master her feelings of ambivalence and wishes to reject her child by showing herself to be particularly giving, loving, and protective, the daughter will attempt to come to terms with *her* ambivalence, worries, and inner doubts by adjusting to the (overt) expectations of the mother and developing into a paragon of (filial) virtue. And on the face of it she frequently succeeds. Again and again we are told that our anorectic patients were particularly good children, above-average achievers in school and sports.

Unlike their more "problematic" brothers and sisters, they never gave cause for complaint. We are told that Petra Landmann was uncomplicated, passive, and rather plump, so here we see the daughter developing a reaction formation that is complementary to that of the mother. But below the frequently uneventful, indeed exemplary, surface of this mother-daughter relationship, we must assume the existence of extreme tensions and rivalries.

SIBLING RELATIONSHIPS

In our own experience and that of others, girls who subsequently become anorectic are not usually only children. Often, however, they may have a sister very close in age. In several cases known to us this sister was a twin. Today we know, thanks mainly to Toman's work (1976), that sibling position frequently has effects on a child's motivation and separation dynamics and on his or her later relationships. In families of anorectics these effects are compounded by those stemming from the family creed and the accompanying binding and (latent) rejecting dynamics.

If the anorectic-to-be is an only child, we may expect the underlying ambivalence and tension in the mother-daughter relationship to be particularly intense. The mother has only this one child upon whom to prove herself as a giving and protective parental person and at the same time only this one child from whom she can (covertly) expect a reward for the lengths of self-sacrifice she has gone to for her own mother and her family. Also, she has only this one child with whom to have a confidential relationship—one that is bound to become much closer than that with the (more and more isolated) father.

If the anorectic has a sister close in age, we may expect that relationship to be another tension-laden, ambivalent one: besides strong attraction, there will be strong rivalry, as in the case of the Landmann sisters. However, because the family creed prescribes harmony and prohibits envy and hatred, the anorectic tries to make the relationship with the sister appear harmonious, friendly, and unproblematic. It is typical for there to have been a history of strong sibling rivalry over a number of generations.

In previous generations this often appears to have been provoked by one sibling feeling unfairly treated by the parents. This applies most often in the mothers' families, it seems. Repeatedly the mothers of our patients made such statements as: "Everything they denied me they gave to her (the mother's sister). She made sure she got everything." Other mothers, while stressing the fairness displayed by their families, were unable to conceal the hidden aggression and rivalry vis-à-vis their sisters. Here we frequently found that the latent anorectic was identified with the sister who had been given preferential treatment: "She could be my sister's daughter," or "She gets on particularly well with my sister."

In general, the anorectic appears constantly preoccupied with whether the sister who (at least in her eyes) had done and still does relatively little in terms of self-denial and fulfilling the parents' overt expectations, is not loved and cherished more than she is. Thus, here too we are confronted with the question of equal and fair treatment, as well as of the possibility of disloyalty and betrayal.

THE ONSET OF SYMPTOMS

Anorexia nervosa normally begins in puberty. But why? The first answer is that this is a phase of development which involves and demands major changes. And these girls and their families find it difficult to come to terms with these changes in a way that will facilitate and encourage related individuation.

The most obvious and probably also most dramatic changes in puberty are physical. The girl's body seems to keep on growing and growing, the typically feminine curves become apparent, and menstruation begins. Very rarely is the kind of girl we are concerned with here prepared for such developments (at least emotionally). The growth of her body, the visible physical changes, the development of secondary sexual characteristics, and the reorganization of hormone balance and metabolism are accompanied by new feelings, new urges and desires, and thus new dangers. This is also a period of vast strides in intellectual development.

The girl develops new reflective potential and the ability to conduct what Piaget calls reversible operations (Piaget, 1950). And yet this new reflectiveness engendered and activated in the course of puberty does not necessarily bring with it any clearer ideas about the things one wants, the things one may or may not do. Both despite and because of this intensive self-absorption, the girl presents all too frequently a picture of extreme ambivalence, seems to have lost her bearings completely and at the same time to be full of contradictions. The literature on this subject is vast (see e.g., Blos, 1962; Lorand & Schneer, 1961; Caplan & Lebovici, 1969).

But the physical aspect and the emotional and mental processes are only one of the fronts on which the adolescent has to battle with changes. The other front, which is of course closely connected with the first, is found in her relationships, both with her parents and family and with her peers.

We will begin with a discussion of the peer relationships, followed by those with parents and family. Today the significance of peer relationships for timely individuation can hardly be over-estimated. For one thing, peers provide scope for learning and experimentation in the interpersonal field. With peers one learns (if all goes well) how to quarrel and make up, one learns to practice solidarity while at the same time developing one's own identity. Then again, one learns to see oneself through the eyes of others, to face up to their criticism and yet to establish and preserve a feeling of selfhood and a sense of one's own value. One also learns, particularly in sexual matters, to regulate closeness and distance, to say yes or no in accordance with the demands of the situation and one's own desires, to withstand the tension of ambivalence.

It is with such processes that separation from the parental home begins in adolescence. Loyalties toward one's family lose their importance; associations with friends outside the family take on a new significance and resilience. There is greater receptiveness for new values, new objectives, new information, encouraging a rethinking of attitudes toward the family creed or, as we put it earlier, individuation *against* the parents (Stierlin, 1983). In short, it is the encounter with her peers that provides the strongest spur to a young girl's individuation.

Such changes appearing in puberty are bound to generate enormous anxiety in the families of anorectics and, at the same time, desperate attempts to maintain stability. It seems that the more the family members have internalized the family creed (i.e., the stronger their mutual "bound-upness"), the more likely they are to see this development as a threat and to make the family as impregnable a fortress as possible, in order to ward off as much of the change, novelty, and disruption of the new situation as they can.

Now it is not difficult to see that, in the end, this kind of embattlement will be of little avail; indeed, prohibiting change as it occurs will aggravate the crisis and militate against a solution of the problems the family is confronted with. But that does not of itself provide an answer to the question why this foreseeable crisis develops into a scenario involving anorexia. To understand this, we need to take a closer look at a number of previously mentioned aspects of the situation in which the girl and her family find themselves.

WHY ANOREXIA?

Here again we first consider the patient's relationships to her peers. Sooner or later the shy and rather gauche young girl will be told: "You're getting pretty hefty around the backside. Why don't you try dieting?" Or she overhears appreciative remarks by her classmates about some other girl's trim figure and general look of fitness. These and other such experiences make her decide to lose weight herself, either by sticking to a planned diet, or by burning up more fat through sports activities, or (perhaps most frequently) by a combination of the two.

Up to this point our patient is hardly any different from many other girls in similar situations, confronted in the context of their relationships with friends and rivals with the slimness ideology generated by the society we live in. The only difference is that the others will be less consistent and less radical in their bid to lose weight.

The motives for such extreme persistence are complex. The most important one, perhaps, is that the totally adjusted paragon of obedience and virtue suddenly discovers here a possibility of proving her autonomy. One of the ways she does this is by going against family values which declare the provision of physical comforts and ample food to be the true expression of genuine love. By restricting her intake of food and refusing to eat, the girl can be seen as rejecting this expression of love, challenging a central tenet in the family creed and individuating *against* the parents. But in doing so, she demonstrates autonomy not only vis-à-vis her parents but also vis-à-vis her own body. The body with its temptations and desires is from now on the adversary to be kept in check. And indeed many of these girls experience sooner or later a triumph of the will in this kind of contest. After the battle against the urge to eat has gone on for some time, we often hear of a feeling of buoyancy, triumph, and gratification similar to that experienced by people who have successfully observed a starvation diet. But this triumph of the will exacts its price. Loss of weight is often accompanied by changes in hormone balance and electrolyte metabolism, with subsequent effects on metabolic processes in the brain and general brain activity. This at least is the explanation offered by experts such as Bruch (1973) for the way in which these girls' sense of reality gradually becomes impaired or is felt by others to be abnormal. This distortion is evident in their insistence that the skeletal thinness to which they have reduced their bodies is normal, healthy, indeed aesthetically pleasing, and that the very thought of gaining even so much as a pound is completely intolerable and repulsive. So it is understandable that outsiders regard this kind of thinking to be a distorted vision of reality bordering on the psychotic.

But a closer look reveals that this triumph of the will is never total. The body with all its needs, particularly the need for food, keeps on invading the patient's awareness. In other words the subject of food continues to preoccupy, indeed to pursue her, and thus to dictate a great many of her actions. These may take the form already described, with the young girl preparing carefully chosen and lovingly prepared meals for her parents and other members of the family, while starving herself at the same time. Thus, what at first glance looked like progress toward individuation and autonomy is seen as something more like a reduction of autonomy and personal liberty. This is one of the many paradoxes that anorexia presents us with.

Other paradoxes become evident when we ask ourselves what effects the various stages of the girl's separation and individuation, all of them implying the necessity (and danger) of change and restructuring, have on the family. We need to remember that this family has little to equip it for flexible reaction to change. It is not prepared for the drama of separation and restructuring triggered by adolescence. In addition, we frequently come across factors that make separation and restructuring even more difficult than they would be anyway. As already mentioned, the parents are often very caught up in a relationship of intense involvement with their own parents. Thus, the time of the patient's adolescence is often a period marked by old age, ill health, and eventual death. The members of such families are particularly likely to assume the responsibilities of having aged parents with an eagerness bordering on self-sacrifice. Thus, at a time when their own children are trying to leave the nest, these parents are binding themselves even more strongly to *their* parents. As a result, death, when it occurs, is a particularly painful event. The parents are then doubly dependent on the support of their children, although they may frequently conceal their need for that support.

The interplay of these various crisis factors does indeed place such a family in a state of increased panic. Family cohesion, and with it general security and safety, appears to be at maximum risk. At the same time it looks as if the parents are about to lose the very substance of their existence, the possibility of caring for their parents and their children. The question that stands between them is: "Can we find a new, joint basis for our married life?" The children, too, ask themselves whether their parents will be able to survive by themselves, anxiously attuned as they are to the crisis the parents find themselves in. A recovered anorectic recalls very clearly how appalled and shaken her father was by a television film in which two 16-year-olds were shown leaving their home and parents. It was then that she decided never to leave her parents.

The parents themselves are suspicious of their children's friends, particularly those of the opposite sex, frequently finding them to be not the kind they "ought" to be associated with or seeing them as a bad influence in one way or another. Here, too, the things the parents actually say—for example, "Of course we want you to do things with people your own age and have a good time"—are often at odds with what they communicate indirectly and nonverbally. The following examples may help to illustrate the ways in which the families of anorectics are thrown off balance by the prospect of separation and the restructuring it involves.

In one family, one of the daughters developed anorexia nervosa just as her older sister was about to get engaged. In another, anorexia made its appearance when the mother, who had lost a son under tragic circumstances, was confronted with the prospect of her second son, whom she was extremely fond of, leaving home to go to university, at the same time as her own mother died. In another family the mother of an anorectic patient was found to have cancer after both her mother and her brother had died of cancer two years previously. Another mother was planning to leave her husband after 10 years of encouraging his progress into total dependence and helplessness after a serious accident. In a further example, the mother had selflessly cared for a number of close relatives of her husband's, including his parents, until their death. When her own mother died, she was on the point of decompensation. And in our own example in Chapter 1, we heard Mrs. Landmann say: "The day my father died, Jutta moved to Cologne and Petra stopped eating."

Hence we see that if we are to understand the factors triggering anorexia and contributing to its development, we require a descriptive approach operating on a number of different levels or, to return to the metaphor we used earlier, a number of different adjustments of the telescope.

The next aspect we wish to consider is the family-wide struggle for power, importance, and attention. As we have already indicated, such a struggle is going to take on very special forms in these families. Power will be invested in the person who is most radical in observing the family creed, that is, the one displaying the highest degree of self-sacrifice and self-denial. And that person is the anorectic daughter, who refuses to eat and generally denies herself more than the others do. This gives her a strategic advantage with regard to the manipulation of guilt feelings, particularly since she is seen, by herself and the others, not as the independent maker of her own decisions but as the helpless victim of a pathological condition. Instituting or enforcing this view of things may not be so easy in her case as it is when "proper" illnesses are involved. After all it was her own decision to embark on the process of weight reduction that led to anorexia. However, this fact can often be relegated to almost total oblivion within the family (quite often with the help of medical authorities) so that the girl is finally perceived by one and all not as a responsible person who has decided to go on a hunger strike but as a sick person, a kind of addict, who must be treated with consideration and understanding.

An outside observer (a family therapist, for example) soon realizes that beneath the continued facade of family-wide harmony and mutual caring there exists massive aggression and hostility. This is directed above all at making others helpless and leaving them saddled with their guilt feelings. In other words, below the surface picture of harmonious complementarity we have what systemic family therapists call symmetry or symmetric escalation, or, as Selvini Palazzoli terms it, a "symmetry of sacrificial escalation" for the status of front runner in the self-denial stakes (Selvini Palazzoli, 1974). And frequently we find it is the anorectic who keeps adding fuel to the flames of this power struggle.

In our opinion there is in many cases a specific reason for it, the realization that there has been disloyalty or betrayal. We have seen that, like her mother or father before her, the anorectic girl has often felt discriminated against, repeatedly attempting to gain the approval of her parents, and her mother in particular, by ambition and achievement. Prompted by the feeling of only being loved ambivalently or possibly even being rejected, she has been particularly anxious to live up to the high expectations of her parents, to display particular affection and obedience, and in general to be as "good" as possible. Now, however, all hopes have gone of becoming the favorite of the parent she has been specifically trying to please. The girl may, for example, arrive at the unshakable conviction that her sister, who (in her eyes) has always had an easier time of it, is loved and cherished more by her parents than she, who, since the onset of her anorexia, has turned into a problem child causing them nothing but worry and annoyance.

There thus develops a revenge dynamic, characteristic of bound delegates (Stierlin, 1981b) who come to realize that all the sacrifices they have made with a view to living up to their parents' expectations have been in vain. Typically, the most effective way they find to satisfy their vindictive feelings is by patterning their behavior in order to make their parents look like failures. They decide to embody the living and unmistakable proof of the badness and ineptitude of their parents as parents.

In the context of this revenge dynamic, the girl intensifies her efforts even further; she disciplines herself even more radically, becomes even more of an achiever, and—the decisive step—cuts down her consumption of food to a point where her very life is in serious danger. In this she is guided by one thought: "However much my parents pressure me and try to control me with their caring, I can up the ante by refusing to eat." Her defiance and frustration usher in a new and heightened stage in the power struggle, the symmetrical escalation: "It serves you right that I won't let anybody help me," or, as another patient put it: "I may be at my wits' end but not as much as my parents are!"

As this power struggle continues and the martyrdom game escalates, the daughter gains more and more power and becomes so accustomed to it that she is unwilling to relinquish it, despite all the sufferings she is inflicting on herself and her family.

In this drama we may see the climax of the conflict that had been latent from the very beginning in the relationship between mother and daughter. Whatever may have started the daughter on her hunger trip, whatever additional motivations may be involved, the daughter's behavior has become a dramatization of the cry: "I'm starving, I need nourishment!" At the same time, however, her refusal to eat and her vomiting are saying: "This food that you're giving me is not what I need, not what I'm craving. I need approval, love for my own sake, affection independent of my achievements." But the parents are unable to decode this indirect and seemingly contradictory message and the daughter is not interested in having them succeed. Hence they react to the radical weight reduction by intensifying their efforts to provide their daughter with food and care for her general physical welfare. And the daughter's reaction is to continue to refuse this care.

Looking at this from a different angle, we can say that this potentially lethal weight reduction means that the anorectic does indeed gain the attention of the whole family, which is what she may have been out to get all the time. But it is not the source of gratification one might anticipate. Although greater attention is lavished upon her and she gains even greater importance within the family, she has to ask herself whether it is only the symptoms she displays that are at the root of this. Only by abandoning the symptoms would she establish whether anything has changed in the family and whether she might still achieve the same importance and attention. Normally, however, she decides in favor of the ambivalent attention guaranteed by her symptoms rather than risk being "betrayed" again and losing her power.

We thus obtain a picture of the anorectic as a person who feels driven to, and justified to wage, a symmetrically escalating struggle on two different planes: She is pitted both against her own physical needs and against the members of her family with their demands that she should eat more. She is fighting against the care shown to her by the others (particularly the mother) and at the same time—and above all—fighting against herself.

Finally, we must be careful not to overlook the positive functions (at least, from the point of view of family members) that the daughter's radical weight reduction has for the family. Daughters displaying feminine curves in puberty represent an unmistakable reference to sexuality, which such families consider dangerous for family cohesion. Fathers who, in many cases, have lost interest in their sexually inhibited wives with their constant disparagement of physical enjoyment, frequently take an erotically tinged pleasure in observing their daughters burgeoning into womanhood. The daughters spark this interest and keep it alive by displaying a kind of childlike seductiveness. This, however, puts them in a new dilemma. They recall the mother's warning that men (and, thus, fathers) are sexually uncontrolled and let themselves go. By losing weight the daughter avoids having to face up to this problem. By staying thin and no longer menstruating, she doesn't present a temptation to herself or anyone else.

Perhaps even more important, however, is the fact that the anorectic's symptoms and the attention she is given because of them reunite the family. There is no longer any question of separation. The parents have a common task and a shared preoccupation again. The tensions threatening to split the family before the onset of anorexia can now be defined as irritations caused by the symptom carrier and her behavior. Indeed, even where the struggle over food has become extreme, we may assume that it is a way of avoiding other struggles with even greater disruptive potential. The symptoms also distract attention from other difficulties. In short, things remain as they were and the family unit is back on an even keel. This could explain the astonishing lack of alarm shown by some of these families when the daughter loses weight so dramatically that her very life is in danger.* The family has regained an equilibrium which is guaranteed durable thanks to the symptoms that have become an integral part of family interaction.

From what has been said so far, it should not be difficult to see why these girls find it so hard to break out of this circle and say: "I'm going, I'm off to work for what I need elsewhere, you'll have to do without me." Pressure of guilt and bonds of loyalty keep them within the family, particularly since they are unprepared to fend for themselves outside and would also have to relinquish the position of importance they have gained within the family. The parents are equally unprepared for a life on their own and believe they need a third person—their anorectic daughter—to stabilize their relationship, to give their life meaning and so make it worth living.

---

* For example, Theander (1970, 1983) found a mortality rate of 18%, Morgan and Russell (1975) reported one of 5%, and other authors found lower rates. An overview is given by Hsu (1987).

5

Families of Anorectics
and Others:
Similarities and Differences

The process of increasing our knowledge involves broadening our horizons, comparing, grasping similarities *and* differences. Thus, in this chapter we intend to look beyond the families of anorectics and consider them briefly against the backdrop of some other "problem families." The same applies to this comparative approach as what we have already said about ideal types; here, too, we are making use of constructions and designs (models, images, metaphors, schemas, criteria) which have been influenced by our research interests and family therapy experience. They do not claim to provide a picture identical with reality.

ANOREXIA FAMILIES AND BULIMIA FAMILIES

The question "What do families of anorectics have in common with others and what differences are there?" poses itself first of all with regard to bulimia. It has only been a short time since

51

this condition began to become properly distinguishable from anorexia nervosa, so we will not be surprised to find that anorexia and bulimia families have a great deal in common.*

In both instances we find profoundly bound-up systems and blocking of family-wide coindividuation and coevolution; in both cases similar, mutually supportive factors that reinforce binding are to be observed, as set out in the preceding chapter. One of these is a family creed emphasizing and consolidating self-control, self-denial, fairness, conflict avoidance, and overprotectiveness, with the overprotectiveness in both cases concentrated around food, bodily functions, and outward appearance. Further, we found in both kinds of families a marked emphasis on achievement, oriented largely toward conventional notions of what that term can be legitimately taken to mean, and finally similarly extreme and polarized "either-or patterns" in thinking, feeling, and evaluation. That means that one either controls one's body or is controlled by it; one either achieves something out of the ordinary or one is a nonentity, a failure; one is either totally bound up with the family or completely divorced from it. There is no third course, no alternative, no "both-and."

Beavers (1985) also found that not only almost all the families of anorectics he knew of but also a large number of families with bulimics belonged to the borderline centripetal families, that is, families in which all the chaotic, eccentric, and disruptive tendencies fermenting below the surface are kept in check by rigid, restrictive, but ultimately efficient control mechanisms.

Families with anorectics and those with bulimics continue to display similarities when looked at in the context of the society of which they form a part. They appear to be units which, either because of their internal dynamics or as a result of external events, have a particularly tension-laden relationship with the modern merit- and achievement-oriented societies we live in. In many cases the grandparent and great-grandparent generations appear

---

* For a description and the differential diagnosis of bulimia, see Casper et al. (1980, pp. 1030–1035), Lowenkopf (1983, pp. 546–554), Habermas & M. Müller (1986, pp. 322–331), Ziolko (1985, pp. 235–246), Mitchell et al. (1985, pp. 482–485), Johnson and Flach (1985), and Yager et al. (1987).

to have been integrated into the network of an extended family, a village community with membership to a number of different associations and societies, all helping to assuage the pain and anxiety caused by the prospect of various stages of separation and individuation within the family. There were always brothers, sisters, neighbors, fellow citizens to turn to for moral and emotional support and, thus, less exclusive dependence on the members of the nuclear family for emotional support and affirmation. But the more this kind of family adopted the achievement ethic of our competitive society, the more it isolated itself from these life-giving roots and found itself increasingly incapable of dealing with the various manifestations of individuation, above all the necessity of carving out an identity for oneself and asserting it in competition with others. This applied to many of the American families with bulimics described by Schwartz and associates (Schwartz, Berrett, & Saba, 1985) and has also proved true time and again of the German families with anorectic and bulimic members coming to us for help. We mentioned earlier how many of these families had undergone sudden wartime loss, separation, and disruption experiences in the parent and grandparent generations.

Where, then, are the differences between these families? A first essential distinction stems from the fact that bulimic patients are usually older than anorectics. One implication of this is that anorectic girls are usually more strongly bound to their families as a result of their age and the stage of development they have reached; a further implication is that the physiological process, which is both a consequence and an expression of recurrent bouts of compulsive eating, vomiting, and laxative abuse, is usually more like second nature to bulimics (i.e., has attained in them a greater automaticity, experienced as being beyond their control) than is the case for anorectics. (Of course, chronic anorectic patients may also feel that they can no longer influence the body's reactions, but even they might cling to the notion that they can achieve a triumph of the will over their bodily processes.) Also, for many bulimics the scenario in which the drama of their constant struggle for autonomy and control, the recurring experience of illusory effort, self-torment, shame, and failure plays itself out is not formed by the family of origin alone, but to a large degree by the peer group, work colleagues, and the "new" family represented by their husbands and (quite often) their own children.

But even in cases where the family of origin is (still) the main setting for this drama, bulimics tend to display greater emotional instability and a more marked tendency to show negative feelings openly (rage, envy, hatred, rivalry), albeit frequently in abrupt outbursts almost immediately suppressed because of the shame they feel about them; separation or divorce on the part of the parents is also more common as is the presence in one form or another of more mature—or, oedipal—sexuality. This is often matched by open bitterness and intensity in the repeated bid for access to the refrigerator and larder, a more overt power struggle also reflected in the aggressive symbolism of the symptom of "throwing up" (Johnson & Flach, 1985).

ANOREXIA FAMILIES AND OTHER "PSYCHOSOMATIC FAMILIES"

Here, two questions pose themselves. Are there such things as "psychosomatic families" and if so, do families of anorectics count as such? In both cases our answer is a cautious yes. However, as we have stressed in other contexts, the term "psychosomatic families" is the designation of an ideal type, a construction designed to give us a first foothold on the way to a comparative analysis, because of the many transitional and hybrid forms, the multiplicity of interrelated features that the family therapist will encounter.

At any rate, once Minuchin and his associates had established the typical features of a family with anorectics mentioned earlier— enmeshment, overprotectiveness, rigidity, conflict avoidance—these were frequently taken to be pathognomonic for psychosomatic families in general. Minuchin and his colleagues went on to discover such features in families where children had developed asthma and certain forms of diabetes, and other researchers observed them in families whose members suffered from such ailments as colitis ulcerosa, Crohn's disease, stomach ulcers, allergic dermatitis, and other illnesses thought to be psychosomatic (Minuchin et al., 1978; Wirsching & Stierlin, 1982).

Today, the picture is rather more complicated. For one thing, the clear-cut distinction between psychosomatic conditions and "genuine" organic illnesses has become more and more difficult to make; also, to the extent that more diverse family groups have been studied, longer time spans have been considered, and more varied and sophisticated diagnostic instruments have been used, it has become more and more difficult to speak of *the* psychosomatic family. For example, in a sample of 55 closely studied families with youngsters suffering from severe chronic psychosomatic disorders, Wirsching and Stierlin (1982) found that only about half fitted into the model of a psychosomatic family as described by Minuchin and his colleagues (1978).

Our own clinical work has, however, repeatedly confirmed us in our opinion that the families of many anorectics do indeed display major similarities to a broad spectrum of families with a record of chronic psychosomatic disorders over a number of generations, or perhaps more accurately, with a record of disorders in which (in our view) psychosocial factors play a significant role. These include not only families with "established" psychosomatic conditions, like bronchial asthma, high blood pressure, migraine, colitis ulcerosa, and so forth, but also a number of others with a record of recurrent and chronic cases of cancer and circulatory and metabolic disorders. In these families we also repeatedly encountered family creeds and relational patterns similar to those we have described as typical of families with anorectics. And we were struck again and again by the frequency with which in the anorexia families we have treated such disorders manifested themselves both in the parent and grandparent generations.

Yet there are differences to be observed between families of anorectics and other psychosomatic families. Probably the most significant difference is that at the beginning of anorexia nervosa we find an act of will, the decision of a family member to reduce food intake, the decision not to eat. Hence there is uncertainty from the outset about whether we are in fact dealing with an "illness" in the customary sense. It is partly a consequence of this decision that the subsequent events take on a dramatic quality generally absent from other chronically psychosomatic families, where we tend to find not a dramatic course of events careering toward some kind of climax but rather, apathy, a scenario of dumb despair, an atmosphere of helplessness and hopelessness hardly conducive to dramatic interactions revolving around the anorectic girl's hunger strike. In short, the drama of anorexia nervosa is an expression of energies and forces that would allow a comparatively favorable prognosis with regard to the patient's ability to manage her own life and succeed with the process of individuation, if only those forces could be properly harnessed.

ANOREXIA FAMILIES AND "SCHIZO-PRESENT" FAMILIES

As set out elsewhere (Stierlin, 1983), schizo-present families can also be regarded as very strongly bound-up systems in which coindividuation and coevolution have come to a standstill. This happens against the background of an excessively blurry, ill-defined relational framework. The members avoid working out a consensus on the basic assumptions, values, and expectations shared by them. This refusal manifests itself in a family climate of constant shifting of ground, disqualification of others' messages, and permanent double-binding strategies. The "softening" of relational reality guards most strongly against what we have called "individuation against," a clear-cut and consistent demarcation of self vis-à-vis the positions, expectations, feelings, and so forth, of the other members, a demarcation that is a prerequisite of successful related individuation.

Selvini Palazzoli (1974) and her colleagues have pointed out that members of anorexia families tend to constantly reject the messages of other members. We feel that this "rejection" is of a different quality from the disqualification of messages and thwarting of the consensus-seeking process found in schizo-present families. Families of anorectics—indeed, psychosomatic families in general—are, on the whole, characterized by an excessively hard-edged kind of reality, where the problem is not so much vagueness as an uncompromising family creed making it difficult to use such evasive and disqualifying strategies.

Yet we have ourselves experienced cases in which, before our very eyes as it were, schizo-present families undergoing family therapy were transformed into "psychosomatic" families; and we have also seen certain families of anorectics gravitate toward the spectrum of schizo-present families.* This will perhaps make it easier to understand why a small percentage of anorectics (also) display more or less markedly schizophrenic symptoms (Hsu et al., 1981). (This was, however, especially true of the relatively small number of male anorectics we have been in contact with.)

---

* These observations support the view that ideal types such as "anorexia family" or "schizo-present family" do not represent typical families but typical patterns of relationship that may change—sometimes very quickly—if new rules, values, and reality constellations bring with them different modes of interaction.

6

Introduction to the Principles and Procedures of Systemic Therapy

In the following chapters we refer repeatedly to the principles and procedures of systemic therapy. For the sake of convenience, we recap them briefly here, although they will be familiar to many readers. We focus in particular on circular questioning, which has developed into our most important therapeutic (and diagnostic) tool.

THE BASIC ASSUMPTIONS

Systemic therapy stems from the findings of modern systems sciences such as cybernetics, systems and control theory, information and communication theory, and game theory. This approach has been used most consistently for therapeutic purposes by the Palo Alto group (Bateson, 1972, 1979; Bateson et al., 1956; Fisch, Weakland, & Segal, 1982; Haley, 1963, 1976; Watzlawick et al., 1974), and the Milan group (Boscolo et al., 1987; Selvini

59

Palazzoli et al., 1978). Traditional assumptions were queried, psychic disorders and illness were seen from a new angle, and innovative therapeutic procedures were developed.

The following account of the basic assumptions underlying systemic therapy is not exhaustive. We have focused on those most important for our present purposes.

1. In this approach attention is given not to isolated phenomena reified and objectified by language concepts but to interrelationships. Thus, individual properties or characteristics ("Mary is anorectic" or "Mary has anorexia") "dissolve" into elements in a dynamic process and are revealed as behavioral contributions to a system and as both expressions and consequences of context-bound labels and attributions. Within such a (systemic and dynamic) view the above attributions could then develop into the following formulation: "Whenever father is urging Maria to eat more, while mother is protecting her and her sister is sending reproachful glances, Maria refuses any further food."

2. A perspective concentrating on interrelationships gives us a new slant on the processes we are dealing with. We no longer construct one-dimensional cause-and-effect chains (linear causality) but attempt to describe how modes of behavior condition each other reciprocally (circularity or recursiveness). This circular understanding of relational processes derived largely from the application of cybernetic thinking to psychosocial systems and is associated particularly with Bateson (1972, 1979). However, Bateson had his precursors, some of them in Germany. As early as 1927, von Weizsäcker, the internist and psychosomatics specialist who finished his active career in Heidelberg, described what he called a "Gestaltkreis" as a "circular process in which the chain of causes and consequences is recursive in terms of the configuration of the event in question" (von Weizsäcker, 1987, p. 184).

Thus, an essential characteristic of living systems is recursiveness—assumptions and modes of behavior rebound or reflect back on themselves. This view not only obviates the dangers of a linear cause-and-effect approach, which is inappropriate to living systems, but also makes it difficult, if not impossible, to stick to one-sided attributions of blame and guilt.

3. Interreacting human behavior forms patterns and is subject to rules. It can only be understood in terms of the context in which it manifests itself. If, for example, a person unfamiliar with football watched a film that concentrated totally on the behavior of the referee during the match, he would presumably come to the conclusion that he was watching a person whose antics were completely and utterly irrational. It takes both the context and the knowledge of the rules observed by the participants to give his behavior meaning. Similarly, behavior labeled anorectic only becomes comprehensible when we regard the patterns and rules determining the course of the various interactions involved.

4. This awareness of the reciprocal and recursive effects of behavior does not mean that a systemic therapist concludes that there is no such thing as individual decision-making capacity and responsibility. On the contrary, we assume that every person is in part the engineer of his or her own situation and not merely victim of illness or internal or external circumstances. Thus, we do not ask: "When did Maria become anorectic?" but "When do you think Maria decided to go on a hunger strike?"

5. Our behavior is influenced not only by the behavior of others but also by the ideas and significant processes guiding and coordinating the actions of members in a system. The more restricted and reified these are, the narrower the scope for action becomes.

6. Ideas about what represents reality are also confirmed, received, or modified via recursive processes. They often function as self-fulfilling prophecies causing problem-solving strategies that reinforce the problem rather than getting rid of it. The more drastic the methods a parent uses to try to change the defiant behavior of an anorectic daughter, the more likely she is to react drastically and become even more defiant.

7. A system is anything defined by an observer as an "ordered whole." By contrast, a problem is anything that a person defines as a difficulty or a source of unpleasantness. This view (of problems) can be individual or shared. We thus ask ourselves repeatedly which system is to be selected as a whole that is relevant for treatment and which persons are to be incorporated into the therapy as problem definers and shapers. In other words, who

is part of the "problem system"?, who are those shaping it through their words and actions? (Andersen, Goolishian, & Winderman, 1986). Frequently it transpires that those outside the family—not least, doctors and social workers, etc.—are also constituent factors in the problem system.

Last, we need to stress that in the last four years theoreticians with a variety of research backgrounds have influenced systemic therapy, among them von Foerster (1970, 1984), Maturana, and Varela (Maturana, 1978; Maturana & Varela, 1980). Probably the most important contribution they have made to systemic therapy is their emphasis on the fact that there is no such thing as a reality independent of the observer. The very process of observation changes what is being observed. In this connection reference has been made to a "second cybernetics" (Auerswald, 1971; Keeney, 1983). The therapeutic context and the relationship between the therapist and the system undergoing treatment are seen as being among the elements shaping the therapeutic process at all times. Hence, in this process the essential thing is to open up or generate realities that increase available alternatives and thus indicate new paths of development (for the individual and the family as a whole).

THE SETTING OF SYSTEMIC THERAPY

The planning and setting of systemic therapy follows from the ideas and approaches set out above. The therapy itself is designed to be relatively short-term, usually, in our case, comprising one to 10 sessions within the space of one or two years. The guiding principle is to provide stimuli rather than to work things through jointly. The stimuli are given during the sessions themselves, the idea being to open up new possibilities of self-organization. The extended intervals between sessions (four to eight weeks as a rule) give the stimuli time to take effect in the life of the system in its natural environment and to trigger problem solutions or structural changes of lasting value for the system. We place our trust in a self-perpetuating process of change (with a so-called ripple effect). This process takes time. In addition, reencountering the system after lengthy intervals facilitates observation by the therapist of actual changes in behavior or system structure.

SYSTEM LEVELS AND AREAS RELEVANT FOR EXPLORATION AND INTERVENTION

We concentrate on three interlinked levels of organization: basic assumptions (significations), intrapsychic processes, and interpersonal dynamics. Whereas psychotherapists using a psychodynamic approach tend to concentrate on intrapsychic processes, systemic therapists attach particular importance to basic assumptions and interpersonal processes. In this we distinguish between three main relational areas: the defined client system, the therapeutic relationship, and finally the therapeutic environment, including such factors as sources of referral, individual therapists, psychosocial institutions involved (if any), and so forth.

We now show briefly how these assumptions and concepts can be transformed into therapeutic action. Forming hypotheses, exploration of relational dynamics, and intervention in the system are simultaneous processes which we are separating here for didactic purposes. The last two processes are part and parcel of the circular questioning approach.

Forming Hypotheses

Instead of individually centered diagnoses oriented toward a medical model of illness and regarding the individual as a bearer of disorders or characteristics, we use hypotheses geared to relational dynamics (Selvini Palazzoli et al., 1980b). These hypotheses are founded on a cybernetically based epistemology. The purpose of the hypotheses is not merely to gain information but above all—particularly as they take the form of questions leveled at the various members of the system—to introduce information into the system. The hypotheses are formed from the answers given to the questions already formed. The information conveyed by the hypotheses relates in particular to new possibilities of explanation and action differing from the views and explanatory behaviors up to now evinced and manifested by the clients. A hypothesis ceases to be therapeutically relevant when it is either rejected or accepted. Thus, the therapeutic goal is to be guided by the feedback from the family so as to always be developing new, acceptable relational hypotheses. The objective is, therefore, not to scout around in quest of a "true" hypothesis.

A further function of the hypotheses is to provide a continuing thread enabling us to impose order on the information we have gained (Selvini Palazzoli et al., 1978). At the same time they make it more difficult for the family to maintain its own established patterns or to seduce us into taking part in these patterns. The therapist's art lies on the one hand in validating the clients in what they are accustomed to and thus establishing a good relationship, while on the other hand confronting them in acceptable doses with new information calling into question their ways of thinking and behaving. In Chapter 8 we describe such a process of hypothesis formation in an actual case.

Circular Questioning

In the period between 1975 and 1980 the Milan group developed a questioning technique ideally suited to both gleaning and generating information at the same time. They call it circular questioning (Selvini Palazzoli et al., 1980b). As the term indicates, this procedure is based on a concept of organization of interaction in human systems as a circular (recursive) process (see also Penn, 1982; Tomm, 1987).

If we regard "information" as "a difference that makes a difference" (Bateson, 1972; Simon, 1988), then information can only be generated via a process of differentiation. The therapist selects certain phenomena, places them in relation to each other, compares them, and distinguishes between them. If differentiations of this kind are to make a difference to the clients, it is first of all necessary to be as precise and accurate as possible in understanding their basic assumptions and the resulting behaviors and to attune oneself to them. There is, however, no way of predicting whether the differences communicated will in fact produce effects encouraging the kind of development that should be taking place. The goals of the questions used in therapy are to "soften" rigid objectification, encourage thinking in recursive processes and patterns, place modes of behavior in the context of relationships changing in time and space, and activate resources (i.e., provide new options in thinking and behavior).

In the following, we list a number of the questions we have found particularly useful.

a. Questions about distinguishing features. Once a concept (e.g., a diagnosis or a characteristic) has been introduced, we ask about its opposite (concept or mode of behavior). This at once negates and puts into perspective the concept or the behavior.

Example: What is it that makes you notice that Maria is *not* being defiant? How is she then different in her actions?

b. "Fluxing" characteristics. Individual characteristics appear to us as attributions abstracted from modes of behavior. They suggest stasis and permanence. We attempt to use questions in order to place these characteristics in a behavioral context and hence reveal them as "in flux."

Example: How does Maria have to behave for her father to consider her stubborn? What does your wife do when you think her to be depressed?

c. Contextualizations. We use these questions to imply that behavior is context-dependent. In what situations is a particular mode of behavior (e.g., one regarded as a problem) to be observed noticeably, little, or not at all? Who is then present? Who reacts how? What behavior has what effect? How does this take place time wise?

Example: What does the mother do when Maria leaves the table after meals and goes to the bathroom to induce vomiting? What does her brother do? How does Maria react to their behavior?

What changes are there in the course of things if father is there at dinner?

d. Revealing mutual conditioning via double descriptions. We use these questions to query the validity of linear punctuations and underline the recursive conditioning inherent in behavior. All the participants are defined as agents, and compartmentalization into activators and victims is not permitted.

Example: Maria, suppose you wanted your brother to take sides with your mother and take her point of view even more frequently, how could you get him to? Suppose you, Michael, wanted Maria to get after you even more often then she does, what would you have to do?

e. "Fluxing" accepted factors (e.g., characteristics) by introducing a time dimension. Opening up a time and history perspective tempers the notion that people possess permanent characteristics.

Example (past perspective): When did your mother begin neglecting her own development in favor of her children and her mother?

Example (future perspective): How long is your wife going to put off the realization of her own goals?

f. Clarifying relational patterns. A number of different kinds of questions can be used to clarify notions about past, present, and future relational patterns in the family. They include:

aa. Differentiations—These are questions about differences of quantity (more or less), quality (better or worse), and time (before or after).

Example: Who does Michael get on better with (talk to more often), his sister or his brother?

bb. Scaling—These are questions about quantitative differences in certain behaviors or attitudes of family members.

Example: Who appears most (least) concerned about Maria's loss of weight? How would you rate the members of your family on a scale of concern where 10 represents greatest possible concern and 0 no concern at all?

cc.   Triadic questions—This kind of question facilitates and encourages a perspective on processes and relational patterns from the outside. A person is asked about the relationship of two or more of the other family members. In asking a third party about others' relationships we obtain this person's view and at the same time, via verbal or nonverbal reactions by the others, an indication of whether they agree with these views or not. Those not directly asked can think about the opinion they have heard. If they were asked point blank, the recursive interaction processes to be expected would probably mean that they would feel more strongly and immediately "interrogated" and would thus be forced to minimize the question.

Example of question to the mother: How do you see the relationship between your husband and your mother?

Example of question to a parent: How do you see the relationship between your daughters? When did Michael and Maria quarrel more—before Maria's eating problems started or after?

dd.   Agreement questions—If we ask a family member whether he or she agrees with the assessment given by another member, then we obtain information on agreement or disagreement and hence about their relationship.

Example of question to the brother: Do you think Maria agrees more with your father's assessment or your mother's?

ee.   Questions on changes in relationships—These questions relate certain changes in relationships to specific past events. They create family-historical realities and place behaviors felt to be a problem in a time-dimensional, relational context which can be changed by events.

Example: How did Michael's leaving home affect relationships within the family?

g.   Questions on individual and collective meanings serving within the family as explanations for the appearance of problems (symptoms).

Example: What explanation do you have for the fact that your father developed his heart trouble exactly when he did, three years ago? When did you start explaining it that way? Do you think your mother explains it that way, too?

h.   Questions on individual and family values. These refer to differences and agreements with regard to moral, political, and other values and persuasions.

Example: Who in the family comes nearest to sharing the mother's conviction that one is not put into the world to look after oneself?

i.   Questions emphasizing resources. The language we use often makes us see things in terms of black and white, either/or. We see ourselves as either passive or active, good-natured or ill-natured, egotistic or altruistic, and so forth. Resource-emphasizers are questions we use to demonstrate that other modes of behavior are potentially available but have not shown themselves.

Example: The father is regarded as pig-headed. *Question:* When did the father last show willingness to compromise or give up a position?

Example: The mother calls herself less intelligent than her husband. *Question:* How would your father react if in the future your mother stopped hiding her intelligence?

j. Hypothetical questions. We use these questions in an attempt to open up alternative realities and options. These are the questions we probably use most frequently. Going through hypothetical situations puts into perspective the meaning and importance given to events in the past and acts as a blueprint for the future which can have a recursive effect on the present. It thus mobilizes hope and systematic activity. We may, for example, ask how relationships might have developed if situations in the past had taken a different course or other premises had been valid. Or we may ask how family members would behave in various hypothetical scenarios in the future. These future-oriented questions are aimed in three directions:

aa. What will happen if everything stays as it is?
bb. What will happen if things get worse?
cc. When and in what way would (implied) positive
    developments be likely, conceivable, and desirable?

Examples: Suppose no children had been born in this family. Would the parents still be together? Suppose there were no therapists. What would the family do then? Suppose the parents decide to separate. Who would the children stay with? When do you think Maria will want to get her period again?

Further questions of therapeutic procedure relevant for bound-up families in general and anorexia families in particular are discussed in the next chapter, where we consider specific aspects of therapy.

7

Context, Setting, and Referral and Selection of Families

Working as a family therapist, one has to adjust one's procedures to the given context and the structures and problems of the families encountered. A meeting at a guidance center with a family with a slightly underweight 12-year-old daughter is one thing; treatment of a hospitalized 25-year-old anorectic who has been in a state of cachexia for an extended period and has long since broken off any major contact with her family of origin is quite another.

THE CONTEXT

Although we now largely concentrate on systemic family therapy, the official name of the institute we work in is the Department of Basic Psychoanalytic Research and Family Therapy. It forms a part of the University's Psychosomatic Clinic and is housed in a duplex in a residential area of Heidelberg. The department's tasks combine research, teaching, and care of the sick. The department does not specialize in any particular catchment area, so its terms of reference are relatively general in that respect. This means that it is possible to choose families for treatment. The department has a high reputation within Germany for its family therapy work; the therapists are acknowledged experts and have made a name for themselves with their publications, including a number on the treatment of anorexia families. This reputation, plus the fact that we have waiting lists of families wanting treatment, is an advantage in that it means that we can concentrate on motivated families. On the other hand, we have to bear in mind that when families come to us, they may feel that they are being seen more for research than treatment purposes. (In 1983, one of us [G.W.] founded a small privately run institute in a town elsewhere in Germany and has now set up a practice there as a family therapist.)

THE SETTING

We usually see families with anorectic members with either the whole team, usually consisting of four senior therapists (frequently using the one-way mirror), or at least two of us present. But since we generally conduct between only one and 10 sessions at intervals of four to eight weeks, the cost involved is far lower than such a personal-intensive approach might lead one to expect. Frequently video or tape recordings are made of the sessions. Once the families have applied for treatment with us, they are given information about the treatment setting. Referral may take place in a variety of ways. We insist (if possible) that one member of the family talk to us on the telephone before the first interview. We do not, however, conduct any preliminary interviews with individual family members as this would create a preferential relationship; we see the whole family from the outset. Families applying to the director of the department on a private basis pay for the sessions themselves. If they come to us via the outpatient department of the institute, then their health insurance will pick up the costs. Family therapy is not yet a standard health insurance item in Germany, but many insurance companies do agree to pay for the treatment as they have found that in a number of cases family therapy prevents expensive hospitalization later on.

THE FAMILIES

Given the factors outlined above, certain kinds of families come to us more often than others. We have more extensive experience in the treatment of bound (centripetal) families, as these show greater willingness to attend sessions as a group. In this connection it would be a good idea to investigate whether there are perhaps more centrifugal anorexia families than we realize. The possibility exists that anorectics from rejecting (centrifugal) families, and older anorectics in general, will tend to go for individual therapy and end up in hospitals more often than the clients we see. In Chapter 9 we give a more detailed description of the families we treat. In Germany it is rare for family therapy to be the first option when psychosomatic symptoms appear. Most of our families had previously undergone other courses of treatment, in many cases hospitalization in a variety of different clinics. On average they came to us more than three years after the symptoms first manifested themselves. This often complicates therapy, as in this interim period certain interactional patterns establish themselves and then escalate.

WHY WE HAVE CHOSEN THE SYSTEMIC APPROACH

The systemic approach is one in which we, as therapists, leave the responsibility for change or nonchange resting squarely with the family. This is partly due to the fact that the sessions are relatively few and far between. We do not give directions for change, and for that reason the families are less likely to look upon us as a threat. As we try to behave in a complementary and neutral manner, there is less danger of our being drawn into the symmetrical game being played in the family or of our being incorporated into coalitions. Distinguishing (relational) questions are used to "entice" family members to define their relationships to one another and see themselves as agents (with responsibility). Unlike structural therapists, for example, we tend not to proceed from normative ideas about what a family should look like. There is, thus, less scope for an adversary lineup with families attempting to assert their own rigid, normative ideas. Hypothetical questions are particularly useful in opening up new perspectives and options without pressuring for change.

Admittedly, structural therapists may still feel justified in preferring their own model, since both demarcations between generations and subsystems and dysfunctional hierarchies represent crucial problems in these families, as already indicated. Perhaps it is no coincidence that systemic and structural family therapists have been those with the greatest interest in anorexia families.

THERAPEUTIC STRATEGIES

In the rest of this chapter we discuss a number of principles and difficulties involved in the treatment of binding families in general and anorexia families in particular. In the follow-up chapters, we move on to a description of the first interview, interventions, successes and setbacks in the course of therapy, and finally to the fuller discussion of a number of specific cases.

Therapeutic Tasks and Dilemmas Posed by Binding Families

The most crucial therapeutic task in connection with these families is usually to initiate progressive related individuation. As we saw in Chapter 2, individuation involves demarcation first of all, and demarcation in its turn involves the ability to make distinctions in a new and more sophisticated way. This means that the systemic therapist's function is to make it possible for the members of the family to perceive and acknowledge differences that make a difference. In other words he or she is a specialist in generating categories implying new distinctions (see Simon, 1988).

Hence the therapeutic challenge—and the therapist's skill—in working with highly bound or centripetal systems lies in:

- making differences possible where differences are being avoided;
- encouraging individuation where self-demarcation is felt to be harmful;
- inducing open exchange where exchange is being avoided;
- softening reality constructions where rigid principles demand that everything should be left as is;
- talking about relationships where a clear definition of relationship is seen as an insensitive violation of the internal "moral code" and fairness ideology of the family; and
- achieving an opening in the family's external boundaries (the therapist him- or herself is primarily one of those on the outside trying to encourage the family to unbolt the door), where the outside world is experienced as hostile.

Questions That Aren't Just Questions

Circular questioning has proved to be a particularly sensitive instrument in dealing with these therapeutic challenges. Many of the question categories listed in the preceding chapter introduce differences and distinctions and also imply, directly or indirectly, interpretations. Normally, however, they are not experienced as threatening or as forcing the recipient to commit him- or herself. The patients are free to answer them or not, as they choose. We frequently point out that we will be asking a lot of questions but that the family members are free to decide which of them they really want to answer.

Basically, "distinguishing" questions are minimal interventions. We are in a position to observe the reaction to them on the spot and adjust our subsequent questions to this reaction.

Confirmation and Novelty

In a study on information and open systems, von Weizsäcker (1974) remarked that information with a stabilizing effect on a structure is largely affirmative (confirming) in character, while information with a destabilizing effect is largely novel (unprecedented). If therapists introduce too much new information, it will tend to be rejected, to the detriment of the therapeutic relationship. If, on the other hand, the information is too affirmative, the relationship will develop well but there will be little or no incentive for change. Circular questioning enables us to balance confirmation and novelty as we go along. An increase of emotional tension or resistance, as we call it, can be relaxed via the soothing effect of questions of a confirming nature. If a good, stable relationship has been established and things are proceeding comfortably, then we can afford to ask a few more provocative questions that may open up new avenues. Also, in family therapy we can always switch from one member of the family to another with a new question, thus altering the focus.

As we have seen, binding families often want to be normal. If we ask one member too early on "Who is most likely to have the guts to step out of line from time to time?" and then request a probability rating, this may have a discouraging effect and create the impression that we are encouraging deviant behavior. But if we ask "Who is the most eager for the family to be normal and its members to be ordinary people?" and ask for a rating here, then we have phrased the question in such a way as to stay within the family's usual frame of reference, while at the same time pointing up possible differences on the relational plane. Outsiders may find the many questions we ask disconcerting. Our experience shows, however, that patients coming to us often feel more encouraged and better understood as a result of meaningful questions than through explicit interpretations and overt empathizing.

"No Difference"

In the sessions, "distinguishing" questions on particularly taboo topics are often given evasive answers designed to define all the members of the family as equal or "the same." For example: *Question*—"Who is the most eager for the whole family to go on vacation together?" *Answer*—"No difference—all equally keen," or "We always go on vacation together." *Question*—"If there is one child who talks to Mother more frequently than the others do, who is that likely to be?" *Answer*—"My wife treats all the children alike." The family's fairness mythology forbids distinctions and the prevailing "we-mode" prohibits deviating responses on issues crucial to the family creed.

Insistent questions about differences and distinctions frequently cause a shifting of focus and increased evasion. Loyalty as a binding factor must not be underrated. Hence we start by asking about "minor" differences or we ask hypothetical questions that do not provoke such feelings of guilt because they refer to things which don't really exist. For example, "If there was a temporary period when one child was emotionally somewhat closer to one of the parents, when was it?" or "When do you think the first time will be that one of the children will not go on holiday with the rest of the family?"

We are frequently able to obtain clearer relational information from the children in these families than from the adults. However, care must be taken not to expose them to loyalty conflicts, particularly when they are still comparatively young and the parents may feel accused or "dethroned" by their answers. For that reason it is usually better to respect the family hierarchy and ask the parents first. But we take the statements of all the members equally seriously and challenge such parental responses as "That's something that Christel (the child) cannot judge yet."

If the answers show a tendency to become increasingly defensive and unproductive, new energies can be mobilized here, as elsewhere, by switching the topic of conversation to the therapeutic relationship itself. For example, "I've just asked an awful lot of questions. What others could I ask if I wanted Peter to say 'I don't know' even more often than he has already?" Or, more affirmatively, "I've just asked a number of questions about incidental matters. What questions do you think are more important for your husband at the moment, so that we can concern ourselves with them?"

Fear of Separation

Binding forces are particularly strong in families in which past separations (e.g., sudden or unexpected deaths) have been experienced as traumatic and the members have not been able to come to terms with them. This is true, as we have seen, of many of the families under discussion here. There is frequently an all-pervading fear that some such separation might occur again.

In work with bound families, therapists are, understandably, often tempted to try to strengthen interindividual boundaries and encourage and support the children in a bid for autonomy. In doing so they are, as it were, pulling at one end of the rope. However, a family which feels that separation is the worst thing that can happen to it will obviously resist this all the more strongly. In this tug-of-war a therapist is usually well advised not to insist on the stand he or she has taken so far, but rather to go over to the other side. Milton Erickson provides a graphic example of this strategy, an event from his own childhood recounted to Jay Haley (1985). Erickson's father was trying to maneuver a calf into the cowshed against its will. In its obstinacy it could be persuaded to go neither backwards nor forwards. When Erickson's father finally admitted defeat, Erickson retrieved the situation by pulling the calf's tail. The calf then shot into the cowshed dragging Erickson junior with it. We will be returning to the question of how to deal with symmetrical behavior at a later stage.

Questions and statements confirming, and perhaps emphasizing, cohesion are thus frequently an elegant—sometimes, indeed, the only—way of helping a family to "get outside itself." For example, "Suppose, Christine, you wanted the family to move even closer together, how could you best achieve that?"

Occasionally we attempt to open up an external perspective for the family by introducing a fictional observer. For example, "Suppose I asked a neutral observer who has known you well for a long time, 'Is this a family that sticks together or one with pretty loose relationships?' What would the answer be?" *Answer:* "One that sticks together." *Question:* "To exactly the right degree, or too closely?" *Answer:* "Perhaps a little too closely." *Question:* "What would he deduce that from?" or "What would make him say that?" Then: "If I asked him whether the family has become more tightly knit or less since Maria stopped eating, what would he say?" Family members often find it easier to answer such indirect questions, as they are not being called upon to express an opinion of their own but only to imagine what a neutral observer might say.

Positive Evaluation of Things as They Stand

Life is a dialectic process developing in terms of polarities. An active person can only experience himself as active and call himself active when he has seen himself to be both active and passive in contact with others. As therapists we are concerned with activating this life-giving dialectic by bringing the hitherto neglected side of it into play and encouraging its development. However, if we are too direct or too unremitting in our attempts, we usually achieve the exact opposite. All we then communicate to the family is: "Things with you aren't as they should be." But there has been no lack of (direct or indirect) criticism—by themselves and others—in these families; what has been lacking is acknowledgment and understanding of the fact that, given their history and their view of things, they have found the most workable situation under the circumstances.

It is against this background that we must consider the so-called positive connotation (i.e., positive interpretation of the symptom), emphasized so strongly by the Milan group. Frequently, confirmation of the status quo is the only thing that will enable a family to gravitate toward the neglected scope of possible behavior at a pace appropriate to it and without feeling threatened. Hence, in working with bound families, the unbinding process invariably involved can only be instituted if there is acknowledgment of the efforts all the members have been making to maintain cohesion and harmony. Sometimes we go one better than the families themselves, emphasizing the positive aspects of cohesion even more strongly than they do. What frequently happens then is that one member will try to convince us that things aren't that harmonious at all.

A word of warning: positive connotation has become an automatic ritual with many systemic therapists over the past few years. They start off their interventions with: "We are impressed by the way in which you . . .," going on to refer to something so general as to be almost meaningless. How great is their surprise when they find that these half-baked entrées are not greatly to the taste of their clients, leaving a rather insipid taste in their mouths! Positive connotation only ranks as new information for families in which there has been mutual criticism and belittlement. Families who see everything in a positive light and provide each other with almost exclusively positive connotations are far more likely to receive an incentive for change from the voicing of more critical opinions about their behavior.

Staying "Neutral"

From the earliest, family therapists have gone on record as considering their work to only be effective in the long term if they are able to maintain a meta-position. This is, however, easier said than done as the therapist is invariably him- or herself involved in the interaction process. The skill of the family therapist resides in his or her ability to do something that binding families are only rarely capable of, that is, regarding the relational and significant patterns from an outside perspective.

Different schools of family therapy approach this task in different ways. There are those who advise the therapist to espouse the needs and positions of all the members of the family. Boszormenyi-Nagy and Spark (1973) speak here of "multidirectional partiality." Structural therapists tend to switch coalitions so as to escape one-sided, long-term alliances (Minuchin & Fishman, 1981). The Milan therapists also refer to "successive alliances." By this, however, they mean something more like the process of asking the family members questions separately and in succession and thus entering into a relationship with them: "The end result of the successive alliances is that the therapist is allied with everyone and no one at the same time" (Selvini Palazzoli et al., 1980b, p. 11).

In general, systemic therapists attempt to behave in such a way that the family members are not able to surmise from their questions what ideal and principles the therapists are guided by. They also try to avoid anything that might suggest that one member is being given preferential treatment: "By neutrality of the therapist we mean a specific pragmatic effect that his other total behavior during the session exerts on the family (and not his intrapsychic disposition") (Selvini Palazzoli et al., 1980b, p. 11).

Neutrality is often erroneously taken to mean keeping one's distance, not getting involved. But this is certainly untrue of the systemic therapist. As a participant, he or she shares the responsibility for what happens. His involvement is, however, of a different kind from that expected of him by the families. The essence of his neutrality may become easier to grasp if we adopt the concept of a "multiverse," as expounded by Maturana and Varela (1980, 1987). We may then put the matter as follows: Bound families commit themselves in many respects to a universe. The systemic therapist, by contrast, will consistently represent the idea of a multiverse. In so doing, he makes it impossible for any competitive conflict to arise about truer or more accurate views or the truer or superior universe. His message is not "I know better than you," but "there are lots of ways of seeing, explaining, or changing something." This "multiversal perspective" is easier to sustain when working as a team. Four people are more likely than one to display different punctuations* and develop different ideas. Teams of more than four, however, tend, in our experience,

---

* Punctuation refers to "the structuring and organization by an observer of a continuous sequence of events and behaviors. Two partners, for example, perceive and organize their ongoing interaction into various sequences, and each subjectively perceives different patterns of cause and effect, or different structures of interaction" (Simon et al., 1985, p. 284).

to run into difficulties of another kind. The process of integrating the various perspectives and ideas frequently proves slow and troublesome. In such a case it is better to form subgroups.

One thing must be borne in mind, however. All the differentiation criteria introduced by the therapists themselves imply evaluations. Instead of the actual questions they ask, they could equally well ask other questions about other things. What is crucial is that the therapists are not experienced as partial in their relationships with individual family members.

A typical neutrality dilemma crops up with binding families when a therapist either supports the separation tendencies of the adolescents or he attempts to interfere with the parents' efforts to subdue such tendencies in their adolescent children. The extent to which he violates the neutrality principle can be gauged by observing the reactions of the family members.

Adopting the expression used by a particular family member can be enough to threaten neutrality. For example, the father of an anorectic may claim stubbornness to be the cause of her condition. If the therapist then asks, "How long has your daughter been this stubborn?" or "To whom is she particularly stubborn?", the daughter may take this as an indication that the therapist thinks her to be stubborn as well. On the other hand, if the therapist asks, "To whom in particular does your daughter display this independence of spirit?", the parents may assume that the therapist is siding with their daughter.

A therapist also relinquishes a position of neutrality if he either falls in with the conflict-avoidance ploys of the whole family and, say, settles down to a cozy chat with them about trivial matters, or gives them to understand that more active behavior would be better. One general truth we have discovered in our work with anorexia families is that if we violated the neutrality principle at all, less damage was done by implying that the parents were in the wrong. The identified patients reacted a great deal more sensitively, often withdrawing into themselves entirely if they felt we were criticizing or harassing them. It is especially important at the beginning of therapy to gain the confidence of these girls.

MAIN AREAS OF THERAPEUTIC INTERVENTION

Complementarity—Boon or Bane?

In Chapter 4, we described the background and dynamics of the symmetrical escalation of the struggle between the anorectic and the members of her family. We must now ask what therapeutic options are best suited to dealing with this situation.

Once a struggle of this nature has set in (overtly or covertly), there is little point in trying to clarify the positions within it. One reality is pitted against another. Nobody is going to pay any heed to such attempts, since they are all intent on gaining control over the relationship and asserting their definition of the situation. Here it is usual for the therapist to find himself being invited to act as a neutralizing or mediating agent. If he accepts this invitation, this normally only has a helpful effect as long as he is actually present with the family. In any event, he runs the risk of being drawn into this symmetrical contest either as a potential ally or as a referee.

The prime therapeutic need in the face of a symmetrically escalating contest of this nature is to make a different kind of behavior possible. But this does not mean that the therapist should try to persuade the anorectic girl to adjust or the parents to abandon their value systems. The essential thing is for the members of the family to acknowledge each other's specific individuality, to respect each other's ideas, needs, and idiosyncrasies, and to negotiate their relational reality.

Symmetrical behavior is only possible in the presence of opposition. If a therapist behaves in a complementary way, then symmetrical interaction involving him doesn't happen. One example of complementary behavior would be for the therapist to ask for help or draw attention to his neutrality dilemma: for example, "How would your parents react at the end of the session if I frequently told them during the session that they were right?"

If the therapist has indeed forfeited his neutrality, he can take a break and, on his return, admit his error. He can also anticipate the prospect of increasing escalation quite explicitly: for example, "Suppose you wanted the conflict with your parents to reach a higher pitch, how could you go about it?" or "Suppose you, as parents, wanted to reinforce Maria in her decision to go on a hunger strike, how could you achieve that?"

Generally speaking, we can say that it is more effective to ask someone directly what he or she would have to do to make things worse than to ask what he or she could do to make things better. Being able to make things worse means having influence on what goes on. Possibilities of improving things have usually been suggested by a lot of other people—without success (Simon & Weber, 1987). We will come back later to the way we attempt to block symmetrical interactions in the later stages of our interventions.

Ill or Wicked (Stubborn, Defiant)

People tend most often to get caught up in symmetrical interactions when they are bound by strong loyalty ties and also fear separation. And in such cases symmetrical interactions are usually accompanied by mutual recrimination and belittlement. In the families we are concerned with here, anorectic girls are frequently experienced by their parents as being defiant and obstinate, that is, in the final analysis as "bad," whereas the parents are experienced by the girls as being domineering, demanding, and overpowering. This is a further factor militating against more complementarity, that is, the likelihood of the protagonists involved backing down, yielding or falling in with suggestions from the other side.

In this emotionally charged state of deadlock, doctors often prove to be "helpful." They are consulted and oblige with a diagnosis—anorexia nervosa. This brings at least a temporary respite. Its nobody's "fault," neither the daughter's nor the parents'. As long as the daughter is suffering from a mysterious illness, both sides are freed of their responsibility. If the daughter's condition deteriorates, she may subsequently be hospitalized. Here, however, we often find the same kind of struggle taking place as at home. The doctors try to induce the girl to eat and she does her level best to thwart their efforts. Labeling this behavior as an illness proves, on closer inspection, to be of doubtful value. Once diagnosed as a "condition," the mode of behavior becomes objectified, separated off, and torn out of its context; it is declared to be the problem of one single individual. There is no other option available than to delegate this problem to the doctors or other psychosocial experts. Also, the illness label provides the less uncompromising parent with a new argument and this leads to even greater antagonism between the parents as to what kind of stand they should take vis-à-vis the patient: either be understanding and lenient or obstinate and demanding. In these families, sickness is an alarm signal triggering increased care and protection. Yet once she has been diagnosed as sick, the anorectic daughter has to fight even more vigorously against being treated like an infant because of her condition.

In light of this situation, the systemic therapist's task is to fight the "illness" myth. Here again, an indirect approach is used, usually via questioning techniques. These questions are such as to imply that all participants are able to act of their own free will. A person deciding to stop eating can decide to start again: for example, "How would Maria's mother change her behavior if she were suddenly convinced that Maria is not ill and can influence her own behavior?" or "Does it suit your sister better for the doctors to consider her sick or would she prefer it if they thought she could have some say in the matter?" By asking a question like "When did Maria decide to eat less (stop eating, go on her hunger strike)?" we are emphasizing the act of will and debunking the myth that this disorder suddenly just happened overnight. Minuchin et al. (1978) define behavior labeled as sick to be disobedience, defiance, and rebellion in their encounters with the family. In our approach we also draw upon such definitions in our questions, but only hypothetically. Also, we keep references to possible interactional sequences in the hypothetical framework and give no indication that we feel a particular kind of behavior to be desirable.

Eating and Weight—Ringing the Changes

Anyone who has worked with anorexia families knows by experience how quickly the subject of eating and weight gets brought up and strong positions adopted. If we allow ourselves to be drawn into a discussion on this point—usually right at the beginning—and then try to mediate, we soon find ourselves laboring with much the same effect as Sisyphus. In hundreds of family mealtime situations, rigid and recurrent patterns of behavior—injunction, recrimination, escalation—have established themselves as a powerful mechanism. So we avoid the subject of eating and weight as far as possible once we have asked our questions on the recurrent and circular interactions revolving around food. Sometimes, however, we do ask a hypothetical question of this nature: "Do you think your sister would decide to continue refusing to eat, or would she accept responsibility for a proper diet, if her parents decided to place the responsibility for what and how much she eats entirely in her hands?" or "Which of the parents would be more likely to take such a risk and stop trying to persuade Maria to eat more?" or "Could you imagine Maria ever saying, 'I'm going to eat if *you* want me to'?"

We do not agree on a minimal weight that an anorectic has to have in order to be treated by us as an outpatient. This would only open up a situation in which we might be forced to play too much of a leading part, to the obvious detriment of our neutrality. Instead, we pass the responsibility back to the parents, asking for example: "How much weight is Maria going to have to lose before her parents accept their joint responsibility and have Maria hospitalized?"

As already mentioned, it is quite frequent in these families for even a dramatic and obviously dangerous loss of weight to be denied and ignored. In such a case we might indeed have to resort to a question like, "What is it that stops her parents from realizing that Maria has lost so much weight that the results could be fatal?" What repeatedly happens, indeed, is that parents bring up the subject of hospitalization when the patient has started showing signs of progress toward individuation and the therapy appears to be threatening the cohesion of the family. We have often found ourselves forced to undertake delicate maneuvers with anorectics who have been hospitalized on a number of occasions to no avail and have lost so much weight that the consequences could indeed be fatal.

The Patient's Life at Stake—What Strategy Is Best?

Although the mortality rate is dropping, a substantial percentage of these girls do still die as a result of the weight they lose. One of our own patients died of heart failure one year after discontinuation of therapy. Any attempt to deal with the fatality problem depends upon whether the parents display a tendency to exaggerate or play down the danger involved. The anorectic patients themselves tend to deny—at least outwardly—that there is any mortal danger for them. If there is a tendency within the family to play down the risk, we normally anticipate the girl's possible death in our questions: for example, "What percentage likelihood is there for your sister, would you say, of a minor infection killing her in the near future?" or "If it were Maria's desire to make room for someone in the family by losing so much weight and finally dying, who would that person probably be, in your opinion?" or "Could there be a dead member of the family that Maria is trying to declare her solidarity with by slowly killing herself in this way?" or a question put to the anorectic daughter: "How do you think your parents would behave if you died? Would they grieve together or resort to mutual recrimination?" If the patient is in acute danger, then it is obviously time for the therapist to abandon therapeutic neutrality and request hospitalization himself. Therapists treating anorexia families without having had full medical training themselves should insist on regular checkups by a specialist for internal disorders or a general practitioner.

"Inventing" a Positive Function for Symptoms

Family therapists display an increasing fascination with symptom functions: the daughter is holding the family together with her symptoms; the symptoms are a major stabilizing factor for the parents' marriage; the symptoms enable the patient to avoid facing up to the problems posed by her development, and so forth.

This view implies that behavior is purpose-oriented, teleological, deliberate. It corresponds more or less to Aristotle's concept of the "causa finalis." But it must be remembered that although modes of behavior can indeed influence each other, functions are something attributed to behavior by an observer. Bateson underscored this by reportedly saying that mountain lions do not eat antelopes in order to protect the vegetation of the plateau.

It can, of course, make good therapeutic sense to suggest positive functions of symptoms by means of our questions. But we have to remember at all times that we are then not dealing with facts but with possible explanations and reinterpretations: for example, "When your brother went off to university and your sister then developed her anorectic behavior (thus coupling the two events), did cohesion in the family become weaker or stronger?" The father's answer was: "Johann was very worried about his sister at the time and came home more frequently than usual." This reply is indirect confirmation that cohesion became stronger. *Therapist:* "Would Johann have come home equally frequently if his sister had not had eating problems?" *Father:* "Johann is still very attached to the family and didn't want to go too far away. But he was given a place at Frankfurt University." *Therapist:* "How is that an answer to my question? (Later) Suppose Johann made friends or found a girlfriend in Frankfurt and stayed away from home for four weeks at a stretch, which family member would miss him most?" These questions are a way of combining the subject of separation and family cohesion with the appearance of the daughter's symptoms.

Sometimes we use direct questions: "Now this next question is probably going to sound a bit crazy after everything you've been going through. But we're going to ask you all the same. Fred (brother of I.P.), do any ways occur to you in which Maria's (I.P.) behavior may have had a beneficial effect on the family?" Normally such questions elicit initial surprise, if not protest. Of course, we do not expect concrete answers immediately, but we do find that the anorectic patients see these questions as a form of acknowledgment of the contribution they make to family cohesion.

For a question like the following, asked of the anorectic patient, a fairly resilient relationship has to have been established: "What do you think, does your sister feel more relieved or more cheated now that you have the whole of your parents' care and attention?" This is both an attack on the parents' fairness myth and a reference to possible sibling rivalry. Even riskier are questions implying that anorectic behavior may be stabilizing the parents' relationship.

Trust Is Nice, but Vigilance Is Safer

Parents of adolescent children have to ask themselves repeatedly how much responsibility they can afford to give to them and to what extent they still need to be warned of and protected from dangerous situations. As already described in Chapter 4, the parents of anorectics often have good reason to be particularly wary. Various events in their past have often confirmed that the outside world is a dangerous place and that they have to keep a particularly careful eye on their children. There are plenty of examples of the awful things that can happen—the cousin who's a drug addict, the uncle who made a pass at the mother, the mother's brother who was killed in a motor-cycle accident, the female relative who killed herself while her mother was out shopping for a few minutes. As a result of these negative examples and the fear they engender, the following rule establishes itself in many families: "We must always know where the others are." If one of them is away from home, he or she has to call immediately on arrival and ask if everything is all right at home. It is best for the parents to take the children wherever they have to go and pick them up afterwards. Thus the children are exposed to an overprotective attitude at an age when they would be better off having more responsibility for themselves. The children internalize the parents' fears and tend to stay home and avoid contact with their peers. As the anorectic daughters appear particularly fragile and sensitive and also feel most responsible of all the children for family cohesion, their individuation is most likely to be inhibited and they remain the most strongly bound family members. Also they are frequently the ones the mother takes into her confidence and thus they get to hear what a burden the unpleasant events in the past still represent for her.

Our questions are aimed at putting into perspective the rules and tenets cementing the bondedness within the family: for example, "When did your mother start believing that the world is evil and dangerous and the family the one place where one can feel safe and secure?" or "When was the last time you were apart from your folks without automatically feeling anxious that something might happen?" or "From what age will your parents trust your sister to look after herself?" or "How often would Maria have to go out on her own without any negative experiences before she could feel confident that the world outside the front door is not always dangerous but can also be interesting and stimulating?" or "What situations does she have to have been involved in for her parents and herself to feel that their fears have been confirmed?"

Prohibition and Permission

As also discussed in Chapter 4, these families tend to gear their efforts to goals and ideals set up by the outside world. Achievement, repression of desires, and adjustment to traditional norms are, thus, important virtues: "It is better to give than to receive." "You must not let yourself go." "You must control yourself." "Do not draw attention to yourself." Failure to toe the family line will bring disgrace on the family as a whole.

Girls in these families normally tend to adopt these tenets even more wholeheartedly than the others, as it appears that they are communicated largely via the mother and her family. It is thus central to the therapy of these families to attempt to soften these rigid norms, to make them less absolute and more expansive. We pay special attention to the image these families have of the role of women. For example: "Who in the family would be most likely to feel selfish about having something for him- or herself?" "Who in the family is most likely to voice an opinion contrary to the family tradition?" "Who was it in her family of origin that instilled the idea in your mother that life is not here to be enjoyed?" "If I asked your maternal grandmother what men are like and what a woman can expect from married life, what would she say?" "Is there a woman in your family who has satisfied her own personal needs and pursued activities of her own?"

Sexuality is a particularly taboo subject in these families. Whenever we have broached it at too early a stage in the therapy, the reaction has been embarrassment, mortification, horror, or icy silence. But avoiding the topic altogether is not a good idea either. This could be taken as meaning that we are also of the opinion that it's best not to talk about it. We thus attempt to approach the subject gently. For example: "Which of your parents is more likely to be demonstrative about feelings of tenderness for the other?" "When Maria (I.P.) has a boyfriend and needs more information on physical tenderness and sexuality, who would she turn to?" "If in the near future your mother were to be more demonstratively affectionate toward your father, how would he react?"

In cases where the girls described problems they had with partner relationships and sexuality, and we gained the impression that they could not pluck up the courage to confide in people of their own age or anybody else, we have sometimes, at the end of therapy, indicated the possibility of going to see a female therapist we know and talking these things over with her. But we find that many of these girls are quite able to enter into satisfying partner relationships as soon as changes in the in-family constellation have provided them with greater scope for their own development.

8

The First Interview with an Anorectic Family

The first interview is of crucial importance (Stierlin et al., 1980). Mistakes made here may be irreparable; in this case the first interview may also be the last and an unpleasant memory for all concerned into the bargain.

For the therapist, the first interview involves three major tasks which are closely interrelated and only treated separately here for didactic reasons. They are (1) obtaining relevant information *about* the system as quickly as possible; (2) introducing information *into* the system; and (3) establishing a sound relationship *with* the system. Circular questioning, our multipurpose instrument, is an ideal method of fulfilling all three requirements. Within this process—and particularly at the first interview—the process of hypothesis formation as a guide to our further investigations is of particular significance.

INITIAL HYPOTHESES

The sources of our initial hypotheses are (1) information gleaned from phone calls, letters, referral documents, and so forth, and

(2) questionnaires filled out by the parents immediately before the first interview and inquiring into such things as dates of birth and death, profession, religion, duration of marriage, illnesses, and so on, over three generations. On the basis of these data we then draw up a genogram.

From the data compiled up to this point, the therapists then develop ideas about lines of inquiry they might follow and questions that need to be asked. The first question is very frequently: *Whom will we invite to the first interview with the family?*

It is quite normal for this question to arise during our first phone conversation with a member of the family. We inquire whose idea it was to embark on family sessions, who is the source of referral, what the problem appears to be, when the symptoms and difficulties began, and what has been attempted so far. We also ask for a list of the members of the family and information about how many of them live together. As we have learnt that, in anorexia families, the grandparents very often play an important role, we also inquire about them. Do they live in the house or in the neighborhood? Finally, we ask ourselves: Is this fundamentally a two- or three-generational conflict.*

As already indicated (see Chapter 6), there has been an increasing tendency in the last few years to challenge the inclination displayed by many family therapists to stay within family boundaries. Instead, there is greater emphasis on the identification of "problem systems" (Andersen, Goolishian, & Winderman, 1986). In anorexia families we may first of all expect to encounter a dyadic problem system (mother and anorectic daughter). Looking further, we may, however, discover triadic systems (father-mother-anorectic daughter, or mother-identified patient-her sister, or father-mother-father's mother) which are relevant to the problem.

Over the years we have found it best to invite the nuclear family (parents and children) to the first interview, including brothers and/or sisters no longer living at home. Certainly, the

---

* Our clinical experience suggests a three-generational conflict (or game) is more likely the more bound up a system turns out to be. Serious and chronic psychotic and psychosomatic symptoms are frequently a manifestation and consequence of massive bound-upness encompassing at least three generations.

central conflict triad may consist solely of father, mother, and identified patient, but if we invited only these three (often highly "enmeshed") protagonists, it would probably be far more difficult both to obtain and to introduce information than if we are able to talk to, say, the sister who has left home. She is able to look at the events at home with greater detachment and may also be freer in expressing her opinion about them to us.

First interviews with the grandparents present are generally difficult to handle. Grandparents often have very deeply entrenched ideas about the ways things should be and frequently also attempt to maintain harmony at all costs. If we only have two generations at the first interview, then this in itself emphasizes the boundary between the parent and grandparent generation. However, even if the grandparents are not present, we frequently ask a number of questions pertaining to their relationships to the other members of the family.

We used to observe more rigid rules, only seeing the family if all those invited actually took part in the interview and deciding ourselves exactly who those participants should be. Today we proceed more flexibly. We still suggest that the parents and all the children show up and also give them to understand that, in our experience, this is the most sensible and most promising course. But we no longer categorically insist. We may stipulate that at least three members of the family are present but we leave it to the families to decide who they should be.

Illustration of Hypothesis Formation

To illustrate the process of hypothesis formation we now describe an actual case. In May 1981 Mrs. Kilian (age 45) calls and asks for a family appointment. A psychologist at a guidance center has told her about us. Her 19-year-old daughter, Kerstin, has been suffering from anorexia with vomiting for a year. She is 5'7" and weighs 75 pounds. A number of brief courses of treatment at a guidance center, a neurologist, and the psychological institute of a university have had little or no effect. A second daughter (age 13) is said to be normal. When Kerstin's anorectic condition got worse, she dropped out of college and returned home.

Mrs. Kilian emphasizes that because of the claims of the family business, the only possible times for an interview are Friday evening or the weekend. We inform her that we do not work at the said times and that the earliest Friday afternoon appointment that we have is five weeks from now; we are, however, free on a Wednesday afternoon in three weeks' time. Finally, she decides to accept this appointment for herself, her husband, and her two daughters.

On the basis of the questionnaire completed by the parents as part of our intake procedure before the start of the first interview, we establish the genogram below. At this point we ask our readers to go through the information gained in the course of the phone call, to study the genogram, and then to form some hypotheses of their own.

Before the interview, the two therapists (one male, one female) developed the following line of thought: Kerstin's anorectic behavior began in 1980. This was the year in which she took her

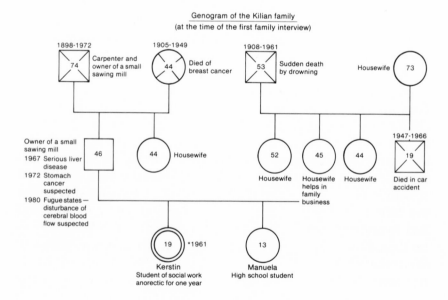

Genogram of the Kilian family
(at the time of the first family interview)

final school examinations and left home to go to university. At the same time her father fell ill (disturbance of blood supply to the brain). After she had developed her anorectic behavior, Kerstin returned home.

Our thoughts centered around the possible links between these events. Anorexia set in after Kerstin left home. Was this separation too great a threat to the cohesion of the family or had Kerstin been unprepared for her new life of freedom and unable to cope with it? Was there perhaps a connection between the father's illness and Kerstin's anorectic behavior? Did the father fall ill *after* Kerstin had left? Was Kerstin perhaps being missed at home as a go-between for the parents? Or had the father's condition (this was the third time he had suffered a serious illness) threatened the family cohesion so severely that Kerstin was returning home, under the cover of her symptoms, in order to restore stability within the family?

In our experience it was by no means rare for a contest for the attention of the mother to develop between two family members. Was this perhaps a family in which rivalry had been sparked off as to who was more ill and hence more needy of attention? At any rate, these were the essential considerations we intended introducing successively into the interview by means of our questioning technique. The reactions of the family would show what relevance these notions had in the eyes of the individual members.

The analysis of the genogram revealed a number of other important things that we decided to keep in mind. Kerstin was born the same year as her mother's father died. Had she, as first child and born close to the time of his sudden death, been exposed to intensive and anxious care on the part of the mother or had she served her mother as a substitute for the grandfather? (This second hypothesis was confirmed later when the mother said: "If it hadn't been for having Kerstin I would never have got over my father's death. I suffered severe depression for months and had to undergo psychiatric treatment.") In 1966 the mother's only brother died in a car accident at age 19. Kerstin was now 19. Were there fears in the family that something might happen to her after she had reached the same age as this uncle?

The questionnaire asks about the grandparents, one of the questions being: "Does he or she live in the same house?" The mother's answer to this was "yes" with respect to her mother, adding "half the week." How did this arrangement come about? Where was grandmother for the rest of the week? Would they have liked to have her all the time or were they glad to be only half responsible for her?

In connection with Kerstin's father we were struck by the fact that his mother died when he was 14. Who had then taken over the role of mother in his family? Or had father, grandfather, and sister looked after themselves? The father had obviously taken over the family business. What did this mean to him? The year his father died he fell ill with "suspected cancer of the stomach." Had the presently threatening separation due to Kerstin's plans to leave home something to do with his recent symptoms? Finally, we had to bear in mind that three attempts at treatment for Kerstin had not succeeded. We raised these questions and tried to transform them into working hypotheses in a 10-minute discussion before we started the interview with the family.

Thus we see that even the relatively small amount of information we had to go on can provide a number of different working hypotheses on one and the same family. Generally one can say that a preliminary discussion among the therapists should not last longer than 15 minutes. The longer one spends generating hypotheses, the more confusing all the different possibilities becomemor else redundancy begins to set in.

SOME GENERAL REMARKS ON FIRST INTERVIEWS

At this point it seems appropriate to introduce some discussion about the conduct and structure of first interviews. As interviewers we are at all times in a position to ask all kinds of questions on all kinds of topics. The topics we concentrate on in a given case depend on our hypotheses and the reactions of the family members to them. It is by no means unusual for us to spend most of the first interview clarifying the context of therapy. But it can also happen that the multigenerational perspective already makes itself felt at this early stage. The speed with which we press ahead with the questioning process is largely determined by the way the relational atmosphere develops. Some families react very defensively to relationship questions or are not accustomed to talking about interpersonal processes with any degree of sophistication. In such cases we remain largely affirmative in our attitude, do not attempt to go too fast too soon with our questions, and may concentrate on behavior sequences. In a number of cases we have invited a family back for a "second first interview." When we do this, we emphasize that we require more information before we can give the family any advice or decide whether family therapy is the most sensible course at this juncture.

In general we use our questions in the first interview to attempt to link up the present with the past, and then also with the future. How far back we decide to go in the past differs from case to case. We have treated families successfully without having to go back any further than the onset of the daughter's anorectic behavior.

Guidelines for Questioning in Certain Areas

In the following we distinguish for didactic purposes certain areas that in reality overlap in various ways. Our presentation of the various elements is, however, still designed to make them useful as a general guide for the sequencing and pacing of first interviews.

As in all other interview situations, we let the family members decide where they want to sit in the room. The results may then be such as to provide some initial indications about their relationships to one another. We use circular questioning from the outset but use direct questions to obtain the hard facts we need.

Explaining the Setting

Before we embark on our questions, we give the family a number of factual details. The families coming to us have a right to be told what to expect. If we tell them, for example, that an interview lasts one-and-a-half to two hours, then we can exclude the possibility of one of them getting up after an hour and saying that he or she has another appointment, thus putting a premature end to the interview. To avoid the impression of any kind of collusion with the original caller, we inform the family members of what we already know. We use the term "consultation" or "exchange of information" for the interview and emphasize that this does not automatically imply that further sessions will follow. However, should this be the case, their number would be between one and 10. Where relevant we inform the family that we have a colleague observing events from behind the one-way mirror, that video recordings will be made, and that there may be breaks within the sessions.

Questions on the Context of the Interview
and on the Expectations for Therapy

In the last few years this set of questions has taken on even greater significance for us. It is a grave error to believe that the fact that a family appears for an interview together means that all its members are equally motivated and equally eager to bring about change. Questions on the referral and treatment context provide the therapists with the background against which the meeting with the family needs to be viewed and insight into the expectations that the family members have in connection with the therapists and the interview. This is not normally an area considered to be in any way threatening, so that the members find it easier here to admit any differences there may be between them. Also, it provides an opportunity for them to accustom themselves to our way of questioning.

THE REFERRAL CONTEXT

The Milan group has quite rightly stressed the relevance of the referral context (Boscolo et al., 1987). One opening question may thus be: "How did you find your way to us?" Probably the spokesman (the "foreign minister") of the family will be the one to reply. We then generally learn who has given the family the information that therapy with us is a viable proposition. We might also ask: "Whose idea was it to come here together?" These and similar questions may be expected to provide insight into what the family members imagine to be the reasons why they were advised to try family interviews and why whoever gave them the advice should have considered these useful in this particular case: "Suppose Dr. X had not been so insistent, would the family be here now?" "Suppose something entirely different takes place here from what Dr. X expects, how would you react?" We also need to know which family members have the most/least contact with the referring person and what influence that would have on the relationship with that person if the therapy were successful. Today we feel that we have learned from a number of mistakes, which can be traced back to insufficient attention to such connections.

Example 1

A female psychoanalyst, who had been treating a young woman of 21 for anorexia over a period of five years, asked us to try family therapy with this patient, adding that she felt she had not been able to help significantly but would continue with individual therapy concurrently with our efforts.

Today we tend to be less wary about conducting family therapy in cases where members of the family in question are also undergoing individual therapy. We include this relationship in our considerations as we would that between the family members in question and an uncle or aunt that they are on close terms with. In this case, however, the psychoanalyst was also the person referring the case to us and we should have been more careful. After the third family interview we gave the family a systemically oriented prescription which troubled the mother deeply. Some days later, she phoned the psychoanalyst treating her daughter (we did not know that the mother had called her on frequent occasions previously) and gave her her personal view of what had happened and a presumably critical appraisal of our closing remarks. According to the mother, the psychoanalyst then advised her ("I had no idea . . .") to break off family therapy under the given circumstances and the mother followed her advice. This anorectic patient is the one fatal case in the sample we discuss in greater detail later. In this case it would probably have made better sense to postpone family therapy until after termination of individual therapy.

Example 2

A 19-year-old woman called us from a psychiatric clinic to arrange for a course of family therapy. She told us she would soon be discharged and would then like to come to us with her family. Unfortunately we neglected to pay the necessary attention to this context. Only when, in the second interview, the identified patient queried the usefulness of family therapy, thus prompting further inquiry into this contradictory behavior, did we learn that the psychiatrists at the clinic (where the girl had been referred by court order) had made a course of family therapy a condition for her discharge. In other words the prospect of family therapy had been the patient's means of escape from the clinic. If we had known this beforehand, we would probably have agreed to interviews in principle but deferred them until after she had been discharged in the normal way. Here it might also have been a good idea to contact the psychiatrist treating her. In general, however, it is rare for us to actively seek contact with doctors and therapists referring patients to us. One reason is that we do not want to be influenced by their assessment of the case; another is that we seek to arrive at a metaposition vis-à-vis all existing relationships, including those with members of the psychosocial professions.

Today we don't usually allow referring therapists to observe the interviews from behind the one-way mirror. Requests of this nature are frequently motivated by a desire to establish firmer contact with us or observe a free demonstration of family therapy from a "ringside seat." Frequently these doctors and therapists are heavily involved with the families and/or identified with one member and hence must be considered as part of the problem system. And that would mean having an important element sitting behind the mirror instead of in front of it. Thus, we normally only agree to have the referring person present if he or she is willing to sit in the room with the family and be exposed to questions we consider relevant. Equally problematic for us are requests by doctors or social workers who are familiar with the patient or the family in a different context to take part in the interviews as co-therapists. In a few isolated cases we have also had the impression that patients were referred to us out of spite, the attitude being, "You're always shooting your mouths off. Let's see what you can do with *this* family!"

Why Us?

Often it is not a matter of pure chance what sources a family look to for help or whether they chose family therapy or a different form of treatment. What the sign says outside the institution where the therapists work and the way their position within that institution is first represented are more relevant factors than is often realized. Age and sex of the therapists may also be significant. Hence it is a good idea to inquire into these matters in order to be able to react appropriately. For example: "What was it like for your father to be referred to a guidance center for addicts (psychiatric clinic, child care guidance center, etc.)?" "What conclusions does he draw from this?" "What is it like for his daughter to be here with two male therapists?"

We have had to realize that the fact that we work in a university institution may lead clients to believe that they are being used as "guinea pigs." For example: "What do you think your mother thought when she saw the words 'basic research' on the sign outside?" "How would your father react if he thought we were interviewing families for research purposes only?" As our department has a national reputation, we also have to ask ourselves whether a family may not belong to the (admittedly rare) species of "big game hunters," acting on the motto, "We've been to

Professor X and we've been to Professor Y and we stymied them both. Now let's see what *you*'ve got to offer (ha-ha!)."

Why Now?

Many families have had problems for a long time. It is thus important to form hypotheses about what has prompted them to choose this particular point in time to embark on family therapy. In one first interview, questions relating to this topic revealed that the parents had insisted on family therapy when it had become obvious that their daughter was seriously preparing to leave home. In another case there were indications of a connection between the idea of coming for family sessions and the recent diagnosis of a cancerous condition in the mother. But the problem presented to us was that of the anorectic daughter.

What Else Have They Tried?

There are a number of reasons why it is useful to learn what the family and its individual members have already tried in their attempt to solve the problems besetting them. It makes a difference whether we are dealing with the first attempt at treatment or whether the family is resorting to family therapy after having tried almost everything else available (family physicians, psychiatrists, psychosomatic clinics, nonmedical practitioners, etc.). The greater the number of prior attempts, the more likely it is that resignation has set in and confidence in psychosocial and medical institutions has been undermined. The experiences they have been through will influence the expectations the family members have with regard to therapy in the same way as the views and approaches of those who have treated them before us will influence the views of the family members. Having the fantasy that we are bound to be more successful than our predecessors usually ends up with the painful discovery of our own limits. Nor are we so creative that we can go on inventing new strategies indefinitely. But if at the end of an interview we tell a family the same things they have already been offered by others to no avail, then we obviously do not appear too helpful: "That's what Dr. X advised us to do in 1982 but it didn't do any good." One of our principles is to avoid critical opinions—explicitly or implicitly—about medical colleagues.

Here are some examples of questions: "What helped most in all the treatments you've had so far?" "What explanation do you have for the fact that, despite all the efforts made by the family and all those people who have tried to help, the family is still not as far along as it would like to be?" "What would we have to do to ensure that contact with us wouldn't change anything either?" "What percentage likelihood do you think your father, mother, sister (you, yourself) see(s) of getting the better of the problem after a maximum of 10 sessions?" "What percentage likelihood do you think your mother considers us (the therapists) to see of that happening? The same for both of us?" "What percentage do you think it would have to be for us to decide to continue with the sessions?"

Who Expects What from Therapy?

One should not assume that all the members of a given family expect equal success and the same results from psychotherapy, in general, and interviews with the present therapists, in particular. Thus, in order to maintain neutrality here too, we ask: "Make a scale of 1–10 for all those present, including us, assessing the attitude of everyone with regard to the usefulness of therapy. 1 means the person in question considers psychotherapy to be very helpful, 10 means that this kind of therapy is totally futile." In general, therapists are well advised to query the usefulness of these interviews rather than to affirm it. Families are then often thrown into opposition; they look for reasons why further sessions might be useful and try to convince us on that point.

An inescapable neutrality dilemma presents itself if part of the family is very much in favor of therapy and the others are skeptical. Here we could be seen as being partial whether we decide to carry on with the interviews or refuse to do so. Such situations can best be dealt with by putting the dilemma back with the family: "Suppose we offered you further interviews. Your father would feel his scepticism was not being taken seriously. But if we refused to go on, your mother would feel rejected. What is your advice?" Or else we split up and say that half the team is in favor of continuation and the other half still unconvinced. Thus we are representing the two sides of this ambivalence.

If the first interview with the family has been preceded by a number of different attempts at therapy, then we use our questions to anticipate the possibility of this in our case as well: "You have had experience, albeit brief, with a number of different kinds of treatment. How likely is it that your brother thinks that this course of therapy won't last very long either?" "Who would be most likely to be in favor of calling these interviews off soon?" "Would you agree?" It is indeed a general tendency that we have to use questions to anticipate what someone might do if we assume that it would be judged unfavorably by the family or have a negative influence on the family's development. This normally reduces the likelihood of it actually happening.

What Does the Family Look Like After Successful Therapy?

The questions probing in the direction described above are, then, first of all designed to point up the different expectations with regard to the sessions. A further function is to prompt the members of the family to develop ideas about the future. For example: "Suppose we had a number of sessions together and the results were satisfactory for everybody concerned. How do you think your mother would then expect the family to look?" The parents usually say that the ideal result would be for the daughter to have shaken off the symptoms and everything to be as it was before. We, however, concentrate attention on the relational changes to be expected.

These questions are also helpful in preventing a therapist from losing sight of everything but his or her own aims and reminding him or her to give due regard, and indeed in many cases priority, to the wishes and expectations of the family members.

APPROACHING THE PROBLEM

The point at which we turn to the actual problems needing solution depends to some extent on the urgency displayed by the family in this connection. It is normally useful to ask about the problems they are up against *at the moment*. If we merely ask, "What is the problem?" we frequently prompt one family member to give us a detailed account of the history of the symptoms. As a result, this person has to be given a great deal of attention and there is the danger of establishing a relational bias toward that person. Another source of danger for our neutrality is a situation where answers to the first questions posed are full of derogatory descriptions of other members' characters or actions (e.g., "Since then Maria has changed completely, and very much to her disadvantage").

A good way to reestablish greater neutrality is to emphasize the context-dependency of these modes of behavior. For example: "What does your mother do when you feel she is overprotective (dominant)?" "Is Maria (I.P.) more defensive at lunch or at dinner, when her father is present?" "Suppose your brother had taken it into his head to provoke precisely this kind of behavior from Maria, how would he best go about it?" Here again, then, we are concerned with softening hard-edged, objectified "characteristics" attributed by family members to one another, gathering different definitions of the problem, and thus placing it in a relational context which is both changing and changeable. In this way, characteristics hitherto seen and described as autonomous and objective properties of the various individuals are shown to be connected. This corresponds to what Bateson (1972) calls double description.

What Happens When Problem Behavior Manifests Itself?

At this juncture we are not so much interested in the family's ideas about the causes of the problems they have to cope with but in the effects—or rather the repercussions—on the members of the various kinds of behavior perpetuating those problems. For example: "What does mother do when Maria appears at the table with a jar of mustard or a carrot? What does the father do, the brother, the grandmother?" The aim of such questions is to introduce the idea that the behavior of the individuals is mutually contributive. In order to try and disrupt the pattern of interaction, which is bound up with the symptomatic behavior of the patient and frequently of a highly stereotyped nature, we ask hypothetical questions aiming to stimulate alternative reactions. For example: "Suppose in the near future your mother no longer appeared so worried, no longer urged Maria to eat, and stopped showing her unhappiness in her facial expressions and physical appearance, what would your father's reaction be?"

When Was the Last Time the Anorectic Did
Not Display This (Symptomatic) Behavior?

As a result of this entrapment in rigid, recurrent patterns of interaction, a feeling of stalemate and stagnation frequently sets in. Whatever is (or was) not as it should be for these families looms ever larger in their perception of things. The future is phased out, possible (natural) changes appear more and more threatening. In such a spiral, situations in which the problematic behavior is *not* displayed tend to pass unnoticed. Thus it is no longer possible to initiate positive interaction patterns. Since this is absolutely imperative, however, an attempt must be made to recall the period(s) in which the symptoms did not (yet) manifest themselves. De Shazer (1985) has provided impressive material on how this can be done. Inspired by his example, we may, for instance ask: "When was the last time all the members of the family felt good for a whole day?" If we then receive concrete indications of such a time, we ask for a detailed description of the way the members of the family seemed to each other in that situation. One possible question to the whole family is: "What explanation do you have for this?"

If the reported situation lies well back in the past or the family evades the thrust of the question by watering down their answer with lots of "buts," we may decide to shift the focus to the future: "When do you think your mother expects it to be possible for her to get back on good terms with Maria and for both of them to respect each other? How would you tell? How would Maria's sister react? What gauge would you have of the problem beginning to disappear?" De Shazer (1985) sometimes refers to a hypothetical fairy godmother who is able to magic problems away: "Suppose a fairy godmother came to you tonight and took all your problems away, how would your husband be able to tell that this had happened the next morning?" If we get evasive answers here, we sometimes direct our questions toward the possibility of a positive function performed by the symptoms; at other times we may switch our track once again by asking individual family members how they could make the situation worse if they wanted to.

Pairing Them Off

Before we can start putting our minds to the way relationships in the family can be changed, we need information on the way those relationships are experienced by the family members at present and how they have developed. The frequently nonverbal responses to many of the questions described here provide clues to which family members are particularly close, thus possibly forming an alliance against someone else.

As already discussed previously (see p. 25), anorexia families avoid clear definitions of relationships: All members must be treated alike, hence preferential dyadic relations are taboo. The following case description shows that it can be a mistake to emphasize and encourage dyadic relationships too early by means of our interventions.

The family included the father (age 49), the mother (age 45), a 19-year-old daughter, and the identified anorectic patient (age 15). Our prescription was that in the next four weeks the family should spend a certain period of each week in varying dyadic relationships separate from the others. What they did together was not so important. At the next session we heard that with a number of modifications they had complied with the prescription (despite the reservations they had about it) up to the week in which the identified patient was due to spend time alone with the father. But that week she was so ill that she lost more weight and the family decided to go out together. In this family the prevailing rule in the triad of "parents and identified patient" was "Nobody is to be odd man out." It became clear, however, that the daughter would have liked to be alone with the father—her eating behavior was far less abnormal when he was present—but felt obliged to display loyalty toward her mother.

It is thus understandable that we often get diffuse and evasive answers to direct questions like: "Which of the daughters do you think is emotionally closer to the father?" So we choose hypothetical questions that are less likely to provoke feelings of guilt. For example: "Suppose in the last few years your sister Maria (I.P.) had been less oriented toward your parents and had done more things with you outside the family, how would your mother have reacted? Do you think she would have reacted in exactly the same way if Maria had gone out frequently with a boyfriend? Suppose you decided to cultivate your relationship with your father more in the months to come, how would your sister react to that? Might your mother then visit *her* mother more often? How would your father and Maria react if she did?" "Michael (brother), do you agree?" We might also bring the frontiers of/ within the system into the discussion by asking: "Suppose you (the parents) decided from now on to close, possibly even lock, your bedroom door at night, how would your daughters react?"

We might also attempt to cast doubt on the mythology of equal treatment for all by asking: "Suppose something convinced your parents that it is important for the development of the family for relationships to be flexible, changeable, and varying, what differences would they display in their actions and behavior?" These last questions are all more or less in the service of change. We would probably not ask them in the order they are presented here but intersperse them with questions implying the desirability of nonchange in other areas.

We also try to learn something about the external perimeters of the family, in other words: "Who has what kind of significant relationship to people outside the family?" For example: "If the mother had something important on her mind and turned to a person outside the family for help, who would that person be?" "What kind of relationship does Maria (I.P.) have to her aunt?"

Anorexia families normally have relatively impermeable external boundaries even before the symptoms manifest themselves. But once the symptoms arise, causing mortification and guilt, the families cut themselves off even more. As a result, the fathers concentrate even more exclusively on their work and the mothers devote themselves even more exclusively to the family. The anorectic girls also restrict their outside contacts even further. Thus the whole family closes in on itself and less and less information penetrates from the outside world. Surprisingly, however, it is not unusual for individual sons or daughters to be allowed freedom of movement and scope for experiments outside the home. An example of a question about external boundaries is: "Who wants most for everyone to be at home in the evening? Make a comparative rating."

What Explanation Do You Have for the Anorectic Deciding to Eat Less?

Looking for causes is normally the search for an explanation that reassures us by suggesting or establishing meaningful connections or consistencies. Another function of an explanation is the attribution of (or liberation from) blame. Experience with doing family therapy shows very clearly how arbitrary and at the same time how important the search for and discovery of causes can be. In the final analysis we "invent" causes by punctuating circular processes in an evaluative manner, that is, arbitrarily declaring some point on that circle to be the starting point of the process. But every punctuation and explanation has different implications with regard to what is identified as a problem and what is a possible solution.

Questions we ask referring specifically to the onset of anorexia are often answered with the following explanations: the daughter has an illness that no one can explain; the daughter was teased about her ample figure and started dieting with other (school)friends; it has to do with her unsuccessful relationship with her first boyfriend; she has always felt driven to do more and more and achieve something out of the ordinary; or, she is just obstinate and willful. Parents tend to see the causes as being outside the family or tied up with characteristics of their daughter. The daughter, by contrast, normally pinpoints the causes either within herself (too fat, feelings of inferiority, etc.) or with her parents (too dominant, "they couldn't get their weight down either"). In each case somebody is to blame and ought to change their ways. Only if it is possible to believe in an illness—or more precisely, an illness myth—is there any hope of being freed from such feelings of guilt.

Here again in the course of therapy we attempt to soften down the hard-edged reifications that have been established and that the family continues to believe in, and to relativize punctuations by placing them in the context of relationships changing over the course of time. Sample questions are: "When did her mother begin considering Maria's behavior to be an illness?" "What explanation do you have for Maria starting to refuse to eat last summer rather than another time?" "What explanation do you have for Maria carrying on with her diet instead of stopping after losing a few pounds, as her friends did?" "Did Maria start refusing food before or after her grandfather's death?" "Do you think Maria would have started refusing food if Christine (her sister) had not moved out and her grandfather had not died?"

"Before and after" questions are particularly useful here: "When were the parents at each other's throats more, before or after Maria decided that life was enough to make you sick?"

But making an explicit link between the onset of problematic behaviors and relational changes is only one of the intentions behind these questions. With certain questions we can both imply that the patient has responsibility for her behavior and unsettle the specific kind of culpit-victim mythology present. The question "When did Maria *decide* . . ." implies that there was an act of will or a decision at the root of her symptomatic behavior.

If the Anorectic Had Wanted Particular
Attention from One of Her Parents, Would It
Have Been More from the Father or the Mother?

We have already pointed out that there is often a connection between the onset of anorectic behavior and the experience of "betrayal." As bound delegates, these anorectic girls have been trying all their lives to obtain recognition from their parents and to give them pleasure by acting in a particularly well-adjusted and friendly manner. But these efforts have, in their eyes, been in vain. In the period before the anorectic behavior manifests itself, they realize that the mother has turned her attention to something else or some other member of the family. The futile rage they then experience is tempered with the realization that refusal to eat is a way of gaining influence, autonomy (on the face of it), and attention. This prompts them to cut down on food even more.

Here is a case vignette. The family in question has five members: the father (age 45, court clerk), the mother (age 43, trained commercial clerk; at present, housewife); Martin (age 19, attending college), Gabriele (age 15, at school, I.P.) and Alexander (age 7, beginning school). At the time of the first interview, Gabriele's anorectic/bulimic symptoms had been in evidence for about a year. We learned that in the nearly two years prior to this, three grandparents had died, the most recent loss being the mother's father whom the mother had been particularly fond of. Both the parents were middle children in their original families. In both cases the older brother had been given a great deal more recognition than they had. In spite of this (or because of it) both parents looked after their parents devotedly until their deaths. Since the age of eight, the mother had felt particularly bound up with her mother because of the latter's "heart attacks" and she also felt restricted in pursuing her own goals. Our first thought was that the family had not yet come to terms with the relational changes caused by the succession of deaths and that Gabriele was distracting the family from the grief process with her symptoms. But when questions and interventions based on this assumption failed to exert any noticeable influence on the bitter, mutual recriminations between mother and daughter, we revised our hypothesis. One other factor that prompted us to do so was the realization that apart from her vomiting, Gabriele displayed a number of other symptoms with which other members of the family (grandmother and brothers) appeared in the past to have channeled the attention and care of the mother onto themselves.

After a certain amount of evasiveness Gabriele did indeed admit that there was something she still wanted from her mother. Our assumption that mother and daughter were locked in a contest as to who should be caring for whom was confirmed. The mother had previously felt neglected by her own mother; at the same time she felt hemmed in by her and constantly at her beck and call. Gabriele in her turn had felt that she came second after her brothers, since they had frequently been ill when younger and her mother had been more preoccupied with them than with her. So when the grandparents died, both Gabriele and her mother felt: "Now it's finally my turn!" Alexander no longer needed his mother so much, because he was now at school and spending more time with friends. When, in this new situation, the mother decided to go back to work, she demanded of Gabriele that she should help to look after Alexander more and that she should take care of her (Gabriele's) mother when she fell ill. Gabriele felt betrayed and embarked on her hunger strike. A pattern of escalation set in.

With younger anorectic girls (up to the age of 13) the trigger factor in many cases appears to be the experience or the acute danger of separation. Depending on the length of time we need to close in on these factors, we then decide whether we should go back into the past at the first interview or use our questions to explore which options and dangers the future may hold.

ANNOTATED TRANSCRIPT OF A
FIRST INTERVIEW WITH A FAMILY*

The following transcript of a first interview may help to show how we, heavily relying on circular questioning, try to achieve the three major goals mentioned earlier: obtaining relevant information *about* the system, introducing information *into* the system, and establishing a sound relationship *with* the system.

The Singer family has five members. Mrs. Singer, 43 years old, is a housewife and works regularly two days a week in her parents' business 100 kilometers away from the Singers' home.

---

* The interview took place in 1983 and the two authors were the therapists.

Mr. Singer, 47 years old, is a top executive in a big corporation. The couple has three children. Sarah, 21 years old, is a university student studying in Italy at the time of the family interview. Sylvia, 19 years old, is the identified patient. She works as a secretary. A short while ago she returned to her parents' home. Johann, 16 years old, is attending high school.

The Singer family differs considerably from the Landmann family described in Chapter 1 (and further in Chapter 9). Sylvia (the I.P.) suffers from a bulimic form of anorexia nervosa. Uncontrollable vomiting is her most conspicuous symptom; her weight loss appears less alarming than that of Petra Landmann. Also, Sylvia had not been an inpatient before attending the first interview. The Singer family appear to express hostilities and conflicts relatively openly, which seems typical of most bulimia families known to us. Such hostilities and conflicts can, to a large extent, also be viewed as a manifestation and consequence of the threat of destabilization experienced by a strongly bound-up family whose children are embarking on individuation. Seen from this angle, the Singer family can serve as another example for the handling of a first interview aiming primarily at quickly establishing a trusting relationship and providing incentives for family-wide coindividuation and coevolution.

After explaining the setting of the interview, the therapists try to clarify the context of the referral and the possibly differing attitudes and expectations of all family members.

Th. 1: How did this interview come about?

M.:   In the magazine *Die Freundin (The Girlfriend)*, we read about an ongoing study. I wrote to these people and got your address, amongst others.

Th. 2: Were these addresses of family therapists?

M.:   No, only of therapists and self-help groups in general. However, at that time our daughter wasn't yet motivated to do anything.

Abbreviations: Therapist 1 = Th. 1, Therapist 2 = Th. 2, Father = F., Mother = M., Sylvia = Sy., Johann = J.

Th. 2: Why family therapy?

M.: Only after calling your institute did I learn about family therapy. My concern was that my daughter should finally make a decision to do something.

Th. 2: How did the family members react to the news that the whole family should participate?

M.: It made sense, I think.

Th. 2: How did the other family members react when they heard that all of them should come along?

M.: My son felt, "Why me? I'm not sick, after all."

Th. 2: How could you convince him he should come?

M.: Most of the time he is quite reasonable. He usually does things when he is told they are necessary.

Th. 2: *(to Johann)* How was it for Father?

F.: *(interrupting)* Unfortunately, we are in the process of moving. Recently, my firm sent me from Cologne to Berlin. That makes things rather awkward.

Th. 2: Then it was not so easy for you to come to this interview?

F.: · We have to return this evening since Johann has to go to school early tomorrow morning. That's quite a hassle.

Th. 2: The more reason for us to appreciate that all of you, except for Sarah, have managed to come. I guess it would have been very difficult to bring her in, too?

(Father and Mother talking simultaneously.)

M.: Yes, Sarah deeply regrets that she. . . .

F.: Over the weekend we've been invited to a family reunion in Switzerland, organized by my parents. This means I'll have to be on the Autobahn tomorrow for another six hours. Again, Sarah won't be with us, unfortunately.

Th. 1: *(to Father)* What do you think were Sylvia's ideas about the fact that the whole family was asked to participate?

F.: What do I think she thinks?

Th. 1: Yes, what do you think Sylvia thinks?

The circular questioning method is employed to elicit the differing motivations and expectations concerning the interview.

F.:   I assume she sees this positively, as an act of solidarity. At least, I hope so.

Th. 2:   One could, after all, have the impression that it is mainly Mother and Sarah who are interested in a joint interview. Could Sylvia possibly feel she is being manipulated into something she doesn't really want?

F.:   Presently, intensive talks are going on in the family. The fact that Sylvia appears to be psychologically unbalanced and is developing anorexia nervosa has caused quite a stir. This is the second or third time this has happened. And that's a major concern for all of us. After all, we don't have any experience with such things. That's something absolutely new for us. It's also difficult to get concrete information. We've looked into the literature and asked acquaintances. Also, the magazine which my wife mentioned has given us some pointers. And the newspapers and media these days are full of information about anorexia or bulimia or whatever they call this condition. All in all, we're confused about what we should do. But apparently therapists are not much better off.

Th. 2:   Sylvia, Mother was active in getting addresses and your sister would also be interested in a joint interview, we gather. How is it for you being here? Did you come because your mother wanted you to or because you yourself wanted to come?

After having first asked the other members in a circular fashion, the therapist finally asks Sylvia directly.

Sy.:   I can't go on like this. It's a catastrophe. It's me, after all, who wants to get out of this mess, but it's impossible. Looking at the future I see no way out.

Th. 2:   Then Johann is the only one who was rather uncertain about why he should come along and who came even-

tually because he was asked to do so? Is it typical that
you *(turning to Sylvia)* are sitting between your parents
whereas Johann has taken a seat some distance from
them?

The first questions aiming at clarifying relationships.

F.:   No, we could easily have another seating arrangement.
          No doubt about that.
Th. 2:   *(almost simultaneously with Father)* Then this is more or
          less accidental?
M.:   There's something I have to correct. That business of the
          addresses was already five months ago. I got hold of
          them, then handed them over to Sylvia and told her,
          "Now you must decide. It's now up to you to take the
          next step. If you really want to get out of this, I will
          help you. After all, you're old enough to decide whether
          you want to get out of this, as you said yourself."
Th. 1:   What does Sylvia mean when she says, "I want to get
          out of this"?
M.:   She means that for quite some time she has been close
          to a physical breakdown. Some time back she was below
          88 pounds. Then the weight went up to 108. Occasionally,
          she was above 110 pounds, only to go down again.
Th. 2:   Johann, can we hear from you about the family's present
          situation? How long has Sarah been in Italy?

*The therapists ignore Mother's offer to talk about weight, eating
and vomiting. Instead, they continue to clarify the family's
present situation.*

J.:   I think since September. She studies there at a language
          school. My father is now working in Berlin. We have a
          small apartment there where my father and I live. My
          mother continues working and comes to Berlin from time
          to time.
Th. 2:   Where does your mother live?

J.:   That's a little difficult to say. Sometimes she lives in Berlin, sometimes she lives near Cologne, where we had our home . . .

F.:   We still own that house.

J.:   (*continuing*) . . . and sometimes she stays with my grandmother—that is in Düsseldorf—because my grandmother's business is in Düsseldorf.

Th. 2:   How much of the time does she live in Berlin, how much near Cologne, and how much with your grandmother?

J.:   I would say 20% in Rosshausen (near Cologne), 50% in Düsseldorf, and maybe 30% in Berlin.

Th. 2:   And where is Sylvia living?

J.:   In Rosshausen.

Th. 2:   She's living there by herself?

J.:   Yes, in our parents' house. She has an apartment in Rosshausen provided by the corporation, and until recently she lived in this apartment. But for the last few months she has again been living with our parents.

The family situation, regarding workplace and home, appears unstable and too spread out. How far does this reflect a phase of transition, of a family-wide destabilization with the wish for, as well as the fear of, a separation?

Th. 2:   How did Sylvia reach the decision to return to your parents' home once more?

J.:   I don't know what Sylvia thinks about this. But I think it was less a decision than an urge. She felt less and less comfortable in her apartment. There were some peculiar characters running around—for example, this elderly man. Isn't that right?

Sy.:   May I say something about this?

Th. 2:   Please.

Sy.:   My main reason for moving back to my parents' house was that my weight was going down fast so that I felt very wobbly and insecure. Finally, I flipped out in that apartment. There was total silence around me. I was all by myself. And I thought that if you have to be alone, then it's better to live in an environment where you feel more at ease. And that's my parents' house, where I spent all my childhood. That place is reassuring, in contrast to the other apartment.

(There follows a description of further changes in the family's working and living conditions.)

Th. 2: Clearly, the family is having to cope with a lot of external changes. How does this affect each of your relationships with one another?

Sy.: We would like to stick together but at the moment we're being torn apart. There was lots of coming and going. That affects everybody in a negative way.

Th. 2: And who, do you think, is affected most?

Sy.: Seen from the outside, it's probably me. And not only because of the move to Berlin. There have been disagreements between my parents for quite some time. There was a time when I'd come to the conclusion that something was going wrong in my parents' relationship with each other. I was about eight years old then. I lost my internal balance. The world fell apart for me. You see, I'm prone to react very emotionally. With me, it's emotions first, and thinking second.

In contrast to may anorexia families without bulimic features, the identified patient in this family can openly refer to conflicts at an early stage existing between the parents. The parents, too, do not appear set on presenting themselves as harmonious and "normal."

Th. 2: Did you try to keep your parents together when you thought there was too much dissension between them?

Sy.: Yes, I tried it again and again. They called me their little homebody. I tried to please everybody and was always running back and forth between them.

Th. 2: Did your siblings react the same way?

Sy.: No, it was mainly me.

Th. 2: Then it is perhaps no accident after all that you're sitting between your parents?

Sy.: *(laughing)* Probably not.

The identified patient is sitting between the parents as an arbitrator and conciliator. This has a dual aspect: On the one hand we can assume that in this way she is feeling boundup, overtaxed, and blocked in her development; on the other, it is likely that this gives her a feeling of power and importance which she would be reluctant to give up.

Th. 1: What impact have the recent frequent moves and geographic separations had on your parents' relationship with each other?

Sy.: When they get together, they quarrel. There are constant fights over trivial things.

Th. 2: If I asked your parents, would they see their disagreements in the same way as you do?

Sy.: I think if they are honest they would see it the same way. We have talked about this quite a lot.

Th. 2: *(to Mother)* Do you agree with Sylvia?

M.: Yes, she is right. My husband and I are not on the same wavelength.

Th. 2: Sylvia shows concern about her parents' relationship. Do you also see problems?

M.: Yes, I also see problems, big problems.

F.: Problems for all of us.

Th. 1: Do you agree also with Sylvia about her statement that these fights have been going on for some time?

M.: Yes. But I wasn't aware that she was aware of them that early.

Sy.: Even earlier than I just indicated. But the decision to do something against it, that came later. I was too young to realize what was happening.

Th. 2: Johann, does Sylvia side more with Father or with Mother when your parents have disagreements?

J.:   Hm, I believe she is still a little more on Father's side.

Th. 1:   Do you agree, Sylvia?

Sy.:   Before, I was Father's child—I don't know for how long. That lasted until I realized that there was a conflict. From that point on I joined the weaker party, and that was mostly my mother because she was the one who took the blows and didn't defend herself.

Further circular questioning with inclusion of Johann reveals that Sylvia, although in the middle between the parents, tends to side with the one whom she views to be the weaker parent.

Th. 2:   When you sided with Father, which side did Johann take?

Sy.:   Johann always kept his distance. At a very early stage he started feeling at a disadvantage in comparison with his sisters. I always got along well with him. That was more difficult with my sister *(laughs).*Looking at things on a deeper level, the seating arrangement seems to fit the situation after all.

Th. 1:   Where would the sister be sitting if she were present?

Sy.:   She would be hiding somewhere in the corner.

Th. 2:   Is that why she is so far away in Italy?

Sy.:   Yes, she takes off, she runs away.

Th. 2:   She likes it that way?

Sy.:   No, not at all.

Th. 2:   Johann, do you agree with Sylvia that it was your experience that when you were growing up your two sisters were more the center of things and you were more on the sidelines?

J.:   I can't remember how I saw it.

Th. 2:   I appreciate your being so cautious with your answers. I don't doubt you have good reasons for this. However, I would be interested to know where you belong in this family.

M.:   He doesn't want to hurt anybody. I would say he is more Mother's boy.

F.:   *(to Johann)* You should say openly what you think. That's why we're here. Everybody should say what he thinks and feels.

Th. 2:   *(to Mother)* How do you see Johann's relationship with his father? At the moment, the two are spending a good deal of time together.

M.:   I would say that things have gotten less tense between them. Before, Johann used to be quite fearful. He was often running after me for reassurance. I would say to him, "Johann, you're a big boy. You can tell your father—he's not going to eat you." But after Johann started his karate training, he gained more self-confidence.

F.:   But that doesn't mean that we beat the hell out of one another.

More questions concerning the relationships of the siblings with the parents and the parents' relationship with each other. How strong is the sibling rivalry.

Th. 1:   Does Father do similar things?

F.:   No, I just jog occasionally and go sailing in the summer.

M.:   My husband used to be a tireless athlete.

F.:   Yes, I was quite active in sports.

M.:   And deep down he's disappointed that the children have not carried on along these lines.

F.:   No, that's not true.

Sy.:   Yes, it is; yes, it is!

M.:   When they were young, the children had sports interests. But that stopped when they became adolescents.

F.:   They only occasionally did some gymnastics.

Th. 1:   This sounds to me as if you wanted to say: "In this family none of the three children had a very stable position." Who do you think got the best deal?

Sy.:   If you're talking about spoiling, it was me.

Th. 2:   Does Sarah belong more to Father or to Mother?

(We learn that Sarah tended more toward father, that she tried hard to win his acceptance, but that she also had also furious fights with him.)

Th. 2:   Sylvia, you said that earlier you saw Mother as the weaker one and Father as the one more able to get his point across. Who do you think is coping better with the present situation?

Sy.:   Outwardly, my father. Even as a child he was able to turn off his feelings—at least, that's what I assume on the basis of old stories about him. He is the type of a man who keeps his emotions bottled up. He works them off by immersing himself in his work. Or, more accurately, he distracts himself. My mother, by contrast, is very emotional. She often cries. She has often come to me to confide in me. She shows much more than my father.

Th. 2:   Who in the family would be most likely to think that Father is in no worse a spot than Mother?

With this question, Th. 2 is again focusing on the parents' fighting and Sylvia's position in this fight. By implying in his question that father might also be having a miserable time, the therapist introduces new information into the system; that is, the father is no better off than the mother. A question of this sort may be used to affirm or reestablish a therapist's neutrality, should this be necessary.

Sy.:   Which of the family members?
Th. 1:   Yes.
Sy.:   I don't know whether they have any thoughts about this. My sister would probably say that Mother is worse off but inwardly she would take Father's side. That's what I think.

M.:   At the same time she would tell her mother—that's me—"you only have yourself to blame for this."

Sy.:   Seeing my mother in the weaker position often makes me furious. After all, everybody should have a healthy portion of selfishness.

Th. 2: *(to Sylvia)* When did you decide to start your hunger strike?

By asking in this way how Sylvia's symptoms began, Th. 2 implies that she was and is responsible for her action, that is, for refusing to take food. And he also implies that she can decide to discontinue the hunger strike at any time.

Sy.: In September 1979. But it wasn't a clear-cut decision. I was kind of split, looking with one part of myself at the other. It was a curious thing. I really thought I was two people. I could look at how somebody was sitting there, not eating, and couldn't understand it. It was only two weeks before that a girl had told me that there was such a thing as anorexia at all. Before that I hadn't heard of the word. This girl said to me: "Have you heard this? This girl has stopped eating." My first thought was: "That's absurd, totally absurd." After all, I always liked to eat. Then I read something in a magazine about a more healthy diet and in this way . . .

Th. 1: Did you also vomit?

Sy.: Not at the beginning. Now I sometimes vomit twice a day. A while back it was four times a day. But I couldn't help it. It became an addiction. I run to the bathroom crying, "I don't want to" but I can't help it.

Th. 2: How big are you?

Sy.: 5′ 10″.

Th. 2: And what about menstruation?

Sy.: When I go below 117 pounds, there's nothing. At present I weigh 99 pounds.

Th. 2: *(turning to Johann)* How did your parents react when they realized that Sylvia was losing weight?

Now that the therapists have implied by their questions that they consider Sylvia to be an active initiator rather than a passive victim of symptoms, they aim at "contextualizing" Sylvia's symptoms. They try to place these in the context of the

family members' (particularly the parents') interactions. We hear
that the parents boycott each other when it comes to developing
and applying a joint strategy to cope with Sylvia's anorectic
behavior. This then increases Sylvia's awareness of her own
power and importance.

J.:   They couldn't believe it. Both reacted strongly. My father
       tried force, conflict, and threats, my mother pleading and
       complaining. But both were equally helpless.

Th. 2: Obviously both methods failed. What did your mother
        do when your father used force and threats?

Sy.:   She told him that it was no good that way. "Don't you
       see it's useless?" she said. "Before you can hope to achieve
       anything, you must talk to her."

Th. 2: Does this mean she was sabotaging your father's
        efforts?

Sy.:   In this respect certainly.

Th. 2: And what did Sarah do when Father was pushing Sylvia
        and Mother said leave the child in peace?

M.:   Sarah said she had to go to hospital.

Sy.:   I only remember you two being around me.

Th. 1: And how did Johann react?

Sy.:   He usually kept out of it when Mother and Father were
       involved with me. Apart from that he felt that I shouldn't
       be making such a fuss. *(Johann nods.)*

Th. 2: *(to Johann)* You're nodding?

J.:   That's not all. I asked Sylvia whether I shouldn't slap
       her if she went to the toilet again—we have three in our
       house. And Sylvia's very cool response was "Yes, of
       course." Then she went down and vomited again. The
       first time I didn't slap her, as I thought she would come
       to her senses. But when she didn't, I once very firmly
       hit her on the behind.

Sy.:   *(softly)* Too firmly.

J.:   For me it was not firmly enough. She started to cry and
       made a big fuss. But I don't think that she was hurt. She
       was only shocked.

Th. 2: Did it have an effect on you—her starting to cry? Did you leave off telling her to stop making such a fuss?

J.: Yes, I told her to stop making a big show of herself but then my father used his authority and told me if I did that a second time I'd have something coming to me.

Th. 2: So if anyone in the family tries to set limits, another one will come along and protect Sylvia?

F.: I thought it was nonsense to motivate Sylvia by slapping her. That's total nonsense in my opinion.

Th. 2: Let's assume that at the time when Sylvia started her hunger strike the parents had told their then 15-year-old daughter firmly and convincingly: "Dear daughter, we want you to live and enjoy life. Therefore you must eat." How would have Sylvia reacted to that?

M.: We agreed that Sylvia needed to eat. We only disagreed about how we could make her eat. My husband was of the opinion we should make her sit down, make her open her mouth and . . .

F.: *(interrupting his wife)* No, no, no, no, no!

M.: *(continuing)* . . . and I told him that is not the way to do it. To make a person open her mouth and make another one push food into it. No, that's not the way to do it.

F.: No, no, that's a distortion. There was never any question of forcing her mouth open.

M.: She had to be motivated to eat because she didn't want to herself.

Sy.: Dad, I remember very well how it was in Holland. We were on vacation. Somebody held my nose and you were trying to push food down my throat. I remember that clearly.

F.: *(defending himself)* I can't remember that, that must have been right at the beginning.

Th. 2: Johann, how do you explain the fact that your parents didn't succeed in getting Sylvia, then 15 years old, to eat?

J.: I think at the beginning of the anorexia Sylvia didn't react quite so emotionally. She knew quite well she had found a means of providing our parents with a common focus.

In general it's better for a family member to point out the power of the symptom bearer than for a therapist to do this. Although it is evident (to an outsider) that the anorectic member exerts enormous power, she often sees herself as quite powerless and victimized. Therefore, it might be risky to confront her with her power too early. She might feel devalued and/or misunderstood.

Th. 2:   Great! And how did things go on?

J.:   *(continuing)* Yes, you could say that at first she tried to reunite our parents. But I think once she had developed her anorexia she became less and less intent on reuniting our parents. Instead, she got a kick out of it. I couldn't help suspecting she got an enormous kick seeing how our parents are killing themselves and achieving nothing. Mother was crying all the time and father completely blew his top. And she was sitting in the middle of this with a sparkle in her eyes.

Th. 2:   She made the puppets dance, is that what you're saying?

Sy.:   *(laughing)* Not a sparkle. I was silent, not doing anything.

J.:   I must add one more thing. Her helping wasn't so altruistic as it might appear. I had the feeling that Sylvia was enormously favored. Sarah was rather lazy. For her it was a big effort to clean up her room. But when she did it once in a while, she was still criticized by my father and mother. In contrast, when Sylvia did only a little cleaning, everything was okay. But when I did it, I was told: "Look over here, it's still a mess!"

We get more indications of a rivalry between the siblings, highlighted by Sylvia's ability "to occupy the center" of family events.

Th. 2:   You mean Sylvia is good at placing herself in the center of the family stage?

Sy.:   As far as I remember, I see the two of us getting along well with each other all the time. For example, I helped him a lot cleaning up his room. He was then about seven or eight years old and I was three-and-a-half years older. However, I usually did the cleaning more on my own initiative, whereas he needed to be pressured. That's why my parents criticized him more than they criticized me.

Th. 2:   That sounds as if you were almost too compliant and are now demonstrating and enacting the noncompliant, independent part of yourself.

Sy.:   Yes, that's the way I see it. Since I got this anorectic thing, my whole personality has changed 180 degrees. When I went back to school after three-and-a-half months' absence on account of my illness, my fellow students and teachers hardly recognized me.

As in most other anorexia cases we have observed, the anorectic daughter is the most compliant and most insecure sibling, presenting the typical picture of a bound-up delegate. After having developed her anorectic symptoms, she has apparently become more able and willing to individuate and assert herself with the others. But she does this typically in a way that keeps her in the middle of the family and makes her the hub of family cohesion.

Th. 2:   Does this mean that this anorectic behavior also has positive effects?

Sy.:   Certainly in this respect. Originally, I was very shy and timid. I was always running away from things and seeking Mother's protection.

F.:   I still see her as shy and timid. Yet she has found ways of fighting it. Before, she wasn't able to. She was more willing to help. Now she asserts herself much more directly.

Th. 2:   So is she giving her mother an example as well?

Sy.:   Exactly.

F.:   Well, that's a good idea. It could be a good idea.

M.:   But I'm quite different. Only I can't stand it when people
          fight.
Sy.:   Then you prefer to take a beating.
Th. 1:   Where did you learn that it's good not to fight?
M.:   At home. My father was a tyrant and still behaves like
          one today. Back then, as now, I had the feeling I had to
          help my mother, that she needed my protection.

*The mother presents herself as strongly bound up with her family
of origin.*

Th. 2:   Very well then, when you go home you give yourself
          the same task as Sylvia?
M.:   I still work in my parents' business. Next year my father
          turns 73. Up until now he has focused everything on
          that business. My brother works in it, and my sister too.
Th. 2:   A real family clan?
M.:   Yes; and now it's time for my father to retire. After all,
          a year ago he said he was going to retire, but only if
          Christiane—that's me—replaces him during the transition
          period, and no stranger comes intruding.
Th. 2:   No stranger is allowed to intrude. That's the way your
          father got his daughter back?
M.:   Exactly. It's true. But I must say my father probably regrets
          what he said. I'm no longer so timid. I've learned to
          assert my position and did so as a child already. Basically,
          I was the only one among my brothers and sisters who
          could. Later they all came to me, even my mother. They
          all relied on me to push things through. I was theone
          who had to go to Father.
Th. 2:   This means then that you are not so weak as Sylvia
          thinks? The clan made up of mother's family really sticks
          together, come what may.
Sy.:   And how! Incredibly.
          (Johann is laughing; several people talk simultaneously.)
Th. 2:   *(continuing)* Did your father have a chance after all?
Sy.:   *(shaking her head)* No, never.

Th. 2:   Families that stick together don't make it easy for anybody who wants to move out. Who do you think is the stronger one—you, Sylvia, who are bringing your mother back into this family by providing anxieties and problems, or grandfather, who is trying to lure Mother back to her old family?

With this focus on the dilemma produced by Mother's conflicting loyalties, Sylvia's anorectic behavior appears in a new light. By providing problems and worries, she is helping her mother to stay with her new family and also with her father.

Sy.:   Hm, when you look at it this way . . .

M.:   (*interrupting her*) Well, I don't know. I don't think my father wants me back anymore.

Th. 2:   (*interrupting Mother*) Just a moment, I'd like to hear Sylvia's opinion first.

Sy.:   Well, I don't know who's getting the better deal in this. I'm inclined to say it's rather evenly balanced; but that means that she must be totally torn apart.

Th. 2:   Let's assume, Sylvia, you gave up your anorectic behavior and developed into an attractive 19-year-old young lady and pursued your goals in life with calm inner strength—whom would Mother then feel more bound up with? Would your father still have a chance to win Mother for himself and Berlin, or would your mother rather return to her family of origin?

The therapist's hypothetical question implies that Sylvia can decide to give up her anorectic behavior and to develop normally. At the same time he anticipates possible consequences of such a decision for the family and especially the parents. But precisely this—anticipating such consequences—could give Sylvia an additional push to pursue her own individuation. This would in turn mean that the parents would be under pressure to progress with their individuation. In other words, there would have to be family-wide coindividuation and coevolution.

Sy.: (after some silence) When I think of the last year, I don't have any great hopes of change occurring.

Th. 2: Also, you have to ask yourself whether the way things stand isn't a pretty good compromise. Imagine you decided in the near future to lead more of a life of your own. That would mean that the apartment in Rosshausen would be empty. What would Mother do in that case?

After having anticipated (and implicitly suggested) possibilities for change, the therapist now takes the side of nonchange.

F.: (trying to correct this) I'm not sure what is meant by the question. In my view the apartment is only a temporary solution. Basically we think that the family will move to Berlin.

Th. 2: Who?

F.: The whole family—that is, my wife, my son, and myself. Not Sarah, if we can take her at her word. Sylvia will still have her own apartment. But she indicated recently that she, too, wants to come to Berlin. She doesn't want to live with us—she wants to have her own apartment— but she wants to be close to us. As a family we are still set on buying a big house in Berlin and giving up the house in Rosshausen.

Th. 2: What is your explanation for the fact that Sylvia wants to have a small apartment close to her parents and doesn't want to live her own life in Cologne, Frankfurt, or Hamburg?

F.: She doesn't want to lose contact with her family.

Th. 2: Why is that still so important to her?

F.: Because the atmosphere at home wasn't good. So she wanted to live close by, in her own apartment. And I've helped her to set it up. I've also told her—and that was certainly not a good idea—that I would give her money for her Berlin apartment as soon as she gained some weight.

Sylvia's apartment and her weight are a tightrope act aimed at finding a balance between closeness and distance, dependence and independence vis-à-vis her parents.

Sy.: It was my feeling that my father wanted to buy himself off this way, that he wanted to relieve his conscience. Inwardly I wanted to separate from Father but was unable to do so. At the same time I wanted to help Mother. In the end I was totally at a loss as to where I belonged and what I should do. As it was, he told me once that it would be better if I moved out of the house and that he would give me financial support.

F.: Support in installing herself in a small apartment.

Sy.: I thought that was terrible, such an offer. After all, I was at loggerheads with him. I was torn between wanting to leave and wanting to stay home and when he mentioned the business about gaining weight it was just too much for me.

F.: I had intended the exact opposite when I made this offer.

Th. 2: *(turned to Sylvia)* What is your own explanation for wanting to move to Berlin? Was it more a matter of not being able to cook for yourself or was it more a matter of being needed by your family, particularly your mother?

Sy.: I would say it was more because of my anxieties.

Th. 1: *(to Mother)* How does Sylvia behave toward peers?

M.: Right now, more openly than she has been. Way back we had an open house. Sylvia brought lots of children along and they were all the same age. Sarah had more contact with older kids. Sylvia had plenty of imagination when it came to playing with her friends. But when her anorexia started, that was the end of it. Her friends came but she would tell them she didn't want to see anybody. When I let somebody in, she would just sit there in silence. That turned her friends off.

F.: When she was younger she really enjoyed life.

Th. 2: Did she ever have a boyfriend?

M.:   Yes, and she has one right now. *(turning to Sylvia)* Your
         interest in boys developed relatively late. That was after
         your first anorectic period when you were 16 or 17.
Sy.:   *(contradicting her)* When I had just turned 16, I'm sure
         about that.

*(There follows a short discussion of the impending move to
Berlin. After that the subject of Sylvia's boyfriend is again taken
up.)*

Th. 1:   How often do you see him?
Sy.:   Every two months.
Th. 2:   Is it love at a distance?
Sy.:   *(smiling)* It has been for four months now, yes.
F.:   The romance is fairly new.
Th. 2:   Is it a romance?
Sy.:   No, not at all. I want to make this clear. In looking for
         a boyfriend I've always been looking for security. I wanted
         someone who loves me, who can show that openly, and
         who doesn't back off. I wanted to have a nest to which
         I belonged. And that's still the case. I simply can't imagine
         just living from one day to the next without someone I
         can rely on. I need a lot of loving care.
Th. 1:   *(turning to Th. 2)* I'd like to return once more to your
         earlier question. Let's assume Sylvia decides to pursue
         her own development, would this mean that Mother
         moves in with her folks or would it possibly mean that
         Mother decides: "I'm going to live my own life more, I'm
         going my own way apart from Father," particularly if
         you, Sylvia, help her to assert herself?

*After it has become clear that Sylvia is moving, albeit ambi-
valently, toward a boyfriend, the therapists return to the question:
How would it affect the parents' relationship if Sylvia pressed
on with her individuation including her relationship with her
boyfriend?*

Sy.:   No, I don't think so. She cannot separate.

Th. 2:   What would you advise her to do if you were certain she could manage a separation?

Sy.:   I've already done so.

Th. 2:   The final decision will be with your parents. But from your point of view, would you find it better if they stayed together or if they separated?

Sy.:   My thoughts on this have varied. First I thought I'd like to help them to reunite. However, some part of myself was thinking just the opposite. That part told me: "Maybe you would like them to separate. They are such different people and don't really belong together." And in particular I wanted Mother to state openly that she wanted to separate, because in this way she would also help me, her daughter. But then I told myself: "Maybe you have only your own interests in mind and your interests may be best served if you keep both of them fighting, fighting on account of you." And finally I told myself: "What's the use? Let them do what they want to do. This is a shitty situation, but I can't help it."

Th. 1:   *(to Johann)* Assuming that the situation didn't get any better, which of your parents would be more likely to say; "I've had enough. I'm going my own way and leaving"?

J.:   I'm at a loss to answer that. Most likely, neither Father nor Mother.

Th. 2:   Maybe you, as children, have a distorted view of this. Maybe your parents have found their own special way of living with each other. Maybe there was never any danger of separation.

By means of their circular questions, the therapists have first opened up the possibility of a separation in the future. Now they introduce the possibility that the two parents could manage without separation. This could be seen as an example of how the therapists exert neutrality. To them neutrality means that the family members cannot deduce from their questions any partiality for a certain person, a certain solution, or a certain position.

Sy.:   Yes, maybe we as children have certain naive concepts about how things should be, like the notion of God the Father with a long white beard.

Th. 1:   After all, your parents have been married for 23 years and have stayed together so far.

Sy.:   That's the point I wanted to make. I now think that my parents need each other just as they are. My mother has been brought up to be the soft one, the one who gives in, who flatters my father this way. That's just the way she is.

Th. 2:   Which of the children could most easily respect the parents' relationship as it is?

Sy.:   Johann, I think. Maybe I'm inclined to see too much in things, but I can't help seeing how my mother suffers and how my father suffers. And then I think it would be so much better for both of them if they could separate. But maybe they need the situation as it is, maybe I should leave them to themselves. I don't know.

Sylvia seems to have reached the conclusion that she is needed less by her parents than she assumed but also that she can do less for them than she believed she could

Th. 1:   Which prognosis would Sarah give for her parents' relationship? Would she think it's more likely that they will separate or that they will stay together?

Sy.:   More likely that they stay together.

Th. 2:   Let's assume they separated after all, which of the two would then get along better?

Sy.:   *(pause)* I can't imagine that happening. It will never end up that way.

Th. 2:   But if you allow yourself to speculate for a moment, even though you think it more likely that they'll stay together?

Sy.:   If it came to a separation, both would be miserable. My father would be at a loss.

Th. 2:   How would that manifest itself? What would an outsider notice?

Sy.:   The house would be in a mess.

Th. 2:   He could easily hire a housekeeper. His salary is big enough for that.

Sy.:   Also, his face would show it.

The hypothetical anticipation of possible consequences of the parents' separation makes the subject lose much of its mysterious, anxiety-inducing quality. Scope for free decisions is enlarged.

Th. 2:   If Father were looking for an escape hatch, which would he be most likely to use?

Our clinical experience has told us that by anticipating "escape hatches" such as suicide, becoming crazy, etc., the risk of these things actually happening decreases.

Sy.:   You mean, whether he would kill himself or something like that?

Th. 1:   That would be *one* possibility.

F.:   That would be the worst.

Sy.:   No, that's not a serious option.

Th. 2:   He wouldn't kill himself?

M.:   I wouldn't be so sure about that.

Sy.:   That's because he once told her he'd kill himself if she left him.

F.:   But that was a long time ago.

M.:   (*crying*) But he said it.

Th. 2:   (*turning to Father*) Would this still be a way out for you if you found yourself in a really serious dilemma and didn't know to get out of it?

F.:   I must have been very desperate when I said that. It wasn't blackmail. I was really in miserable shape. But that's no longer an answer for me. When I think back, it coincided . . .

M.:   (*interrupting him, still crying*) It happened repeatedly, even at the beginning of our relationship.

F.:   Well, there were . . .

Th. 2: *(following up Father's previous statement)* You said it coincided with something?

F.: Yes. Four or five years ago, I had some sort of an eye
opener. Maybe that was then when things started getting
on the wrong track. What triggered it off didn't seem
serious at the time. I had the feeling my wife was becoming somewhat overinvested in the children at the
expense of our relationship. Anything the children might
say was so much more important to her than the things
I held to be important. It was then that, for the first time,
I brought things to a head, as it were. I asked my wife
to let up on the children's side a little and to pay more
attention to me. After all, the children were growing up
and could more easily fend for themselves. When I suggested this, she accused me of selfishness. That hurt me
deeply. I was desperate. I asked myself: "What's in this
for me?" In fact I started doubting whether our marriage
still had a solid basis.

*An event four or five years previously brought the different
expectations and needs of the marital partners into the fore-
ground. This was in the context of the children's pending individuation which was threatening family cohesion. Father was
then thinking of suicide and separating from his wife. Now the
question is: Is there still a threat of suicide? To find an answer
one would have to assess whether the marital partners are still
bogged down in an irreconcilable either-or stalemate or whether
there has been some movement in the direction of more family-
wide coindividuation and coevolution.*

Th. 2: Mr. Singer, a moment ago, when we were talking about
suicide, your wife was very moved, as if she were afraid
it could still happen. But if I have understood you correctly, Mr. Singer, then this is no longer an option for
you. The question of suicide arose in the context of a
crisis four or five years ago and that crisis is now resolved?

F.: Since this thing happened, there have been ups and
downs. We've gotten together and drifted apart again.
Certainly, the situation is quite complex and still in flux.

Th. 2:   Are you still in danger of killing yourself?

F.:   No, I can state that categorically.

Th. 2:   Do you think your family can believe this when they hear it?

F.:   They can rely on my word, absolutely. I would say the fire has died down. Things are on a more even keel now. There is more distance, but also less depression. I don't know whether it's better this way. But that's how it is. In brief, I don't see any further danger in terms of suicide.

Th. 2:   (to Mrs. Singer) Would there be still another escape hatch for your husband?

M.:   I would think he might still do something crazy and impulsive on the spur of the moment. My husband is that way.

Th. 2:   (in a slightly humorous tone) You mean he might commit a murder?

(Mother and Sylvia laugh somewhat tensely.)

M.:   I'm not so sure. When he was really furious, he didn't mind what he did if he found something standing in his way. In such situations it might happen the children would come up from the basement with all their friends because they thought my husband was hitting me. But it was only plates flying around.

Th. 1:   What would Mother need to do if she wanted Father to give her a beating?

Such a question, again posed in a circular fashion, implies that the mother is not merely a victim but an active contributor to the drama. This implies further that she is in a position to bring about changes.

J.:   I don't know.

M.:   Today I no longer fear he might become violent. But sometimes I'm still afraid his nerves can't take the strain. After all, both his mother and his sister had weak nerves. When his sister married, this was too much for her. She suffered a nervous breakdown. Evidently, his folks can't take much.

F.:   (agreeing) Perhaps as regards nerves . . .

M.:   Let's take visitors, for example. I don't mind if a visitor
           shows up at the door unexpectedly. But in my husband's
           family everything has to be preplanned. If somebody
           arrives at the door unannounced, everybody flips out.

Th. 2:   Clearly, you come from very different types of families,
           don't you think?

F.:   Very much so, from very different ones. I'm a perfectionist,
           a fanatic for punctuality.

Th. 1:   Before we look further into your families of origin, let's
           hear whether there are escape hatches for your wife, too.
           Sylvia, what would be an escape hatch for your mother
           if she found herself in a really tight spot?

*Neutrality is also indicated when asking about "escape hatches."
Otherwise, one member would be singled out as the crazy or
pathological one.*

Sy.:   She would go back to her own family.

Th. 2:   Would she have a good time there?

M.:   No, I would live for myself. Well, not quite. To some
           extent I've committed myself to working in my parents'
           business.

Th. 2:   (more softly and with a humorous undertone, to Sylvia) In
           a separate apartment close to the parents?
           (All laugh.)

Sy.:   Exactly, exactly!

F.:   *With* her parents or *close to* her parents?

Th. 2:   Would Father pay her for the upkeep of the apartment?

M.:   No, he wouldn't do that.

Th. 2:   Well, let's wait and see!

Sy.:   Mother could also become ill and then stop eating. She
           would simply lie there, vomiting and complaining about
           headaches.

F.:   She also has trouble with her liver.

Th. 2:   It's interesting that you think Mother might vomit and
           lose weight.

F.:   The liver could be a good safety valve for her.

Th. 2:   And if Johann decided to make a mess of his life, what special talents would he have in that direction?

Sy.:   Aggression. He's rather hot-tempered. He went so far as to smash toys which he modeled himself and which he loved very much.

Th. 2:   This means he, too, would act like a real Singer.

Sy.:   (smiling) Yes.

Th. 1:   How do you see it yourself, Johann?

J.:   Well, up to three to four years ago I was still capable of smashing things because of my quick temper. But now I see no more sense in destroying things or hurting anybody.

Th. 1:   Would there be other escape hatches?

J.:   I would train for karate.

Th. 1:   And Sarah?

F.:   Sarah reacts to stress at home by playing the piano.

M.:   Or she would go to her friends.

Sy.:   She would seek company and talk a lot.

F.:   Yes, discuss things a lot.

Th. 1:   Well, we heard, Mr. Singer, that your wife doesn't get along very well with her own family?

Earlier questions concerned Mr. Singer's family of origin, revealing a disposition here to nervous breakdown. Again, in the interests of balance and neutrality, Mrs. Singer's family of origin should also be discussed. It becomes apparent that not only different temperaments and needs but also the conflicting loyalties of the marital partners are making for estrangement in their relationship.

F.:   Yes.

Th. 2:   With whom does she get along best?

F.:   Seen from my point of view?

Th. 2:   Yes. We like to pose questions in a roundabout way.

F.:   Yes. I'm aware of that. Well, I find your question difficult to answer. My wife is a very resolute and dominating woman. Very conscientious but lacking inner harmony and lacking Gemütlichkeit. Unfortunately, in my parental home there was also a lack of Gemütlichkeit and warmth. I've suffered from this a lot. Also, I didn't succeed in developing a warm relationship with my mother. I realize this when talking with my wife. In fact, I've felt much more comfortable in the home of my wife's parents. These are people from the Southern Rhineland. That's quite a different stock. Much more outgoing and I liked that. My parents are quite a contrast. They come from Pomerania. They were more constrained, reluctant to give anything away. Life with them was rather hard and I'm sure my wife didn't like that. We had lots of fights because I defended my parents against her criticisms.

Th. 2: Evidently, you are both loyal children to your parents?

F.: Well yes, but . . .

M.: Yes, for years I was also a loyal child to *his* parents, until I was told that this wasn't wanted.

F.: *(rather irritated)* That it wasn't wanted?

M.: You were a lazy letter writer. Your parents complained that they didn't hear anything from you. *(with irony in her voice)* I started to write a letter every week in order to supply your poor parents with some mail. Finally I got a letter saying certainly, it was nice that I was writing them but they would prefer to get a letter even once a month from you rather than once a week from me.

F.: That hurt her.

M.: Yes, my mother-in-law told me quite openly from the beginning that I was too generous. Again and again she made the remark that I would make my husband into a pauper by not realizing that there was nothing to be generous with.

F.: From her point of view my wife was certainly in the right when she attacked me because of my parents. I also told her that I disliked some traits of my parents. Because I disliked these traits too, I got into fights with them. And now I firmly take my wife's part. Unfortunately, she's seldom given me credit for this. I'm unhappy about these disagreements with my parents. I've suffered from them enormously. I'm still suffering from them. Even today I don't like going home.

Th. 1:   This, then, would be the difference between the two of you: in case of a separation you, Mrs. Singer, could easily return to your family of origin, whereas you, Mr. Singer, would be reluctant to do so.

F.:   Absolutely. It would be quite impossible. I would never do that.

Th. 2:   At this point we would like to have a break in order to discuss matters on our own.

(The family takes a stroll in the garden; the therapists have their discussion in a separate room.)

The therapists' discussion lasts about 10 minutes. They quickly reach an agreement on an evaluation of the Singers' present situation: The children's moves toward greater individuation/separation, as well as external strains (e.g., Mr. Singer's promotion and impending move to another city), have contributed to an increase of tensions and centrifugal tendencies in the family. With that, there has been an increase of anxieties and counterbinding forces. This in turn has augmented Sylvia's dilemma as the one placed (or placing herself) in the middle between the two parents. On the one hand, she too would like to break away from the family; on the other, she is held in this middle position both because she is needed as conciliator and arbitrator and because it gives her a sense of importance and power. At the same time, by behaving seductively toward her father, she further increases the tensions between the parents, which in turn increases her own sense of being center stage.

At first, the therapists think of prescribing the family some homework or ritual but decide eventually to present themselves as split: One is to be the proponent of change, the other of nonchange. The proponent of change is also to provoke Sylvia a little by calling her a princess. They think such provocation might be best suited to motivate her to escape from her princess role.

Final Comments

Th. 1:   We would like to acknowledge all your efforts to making life in this family a workable proposition and, in particular, to helping Sylvia. You have gone a long way toward tackling open questions jointly. When a family has to cope with moves and separations—and these are always troubling times—there is a chance for new beginnings. At the same time, more insecurities and anxieties are usually the case.

   We two have differing views of the family's present situation. In particular, we are unable to agree on how to evaluate your behavior, Sylvia. Is it to be seen more as a manifestation and consequence of your active commitment to the cohesion of the family and the maintenance of your parents' marriage, or as a manifestation and consequence of the role of princess in which you found yourself in this family? I think that you, Sylvia, will most likely continue to carry on in your role as princess. That means you will continue to do your part in keeping up the present equilibrium, which involves moving to Berlin and turning to Father to find an apartment and a job close to your parents' home. I think that's okay, because it could well be that the impending move and simultaneous destabilization of the family represent too many changes in too short a time, particularly in view of the fact that you, Mr. and Mrs. Singer, are not certain about how you want to go on with your relationship.

Th. 2:   I, in contrast, think it possible, even probable, that you, Sylvia, and you, Mr. and Mrs. Singer, will use the situation for a new orientation. It is my assumption that you, Sylvia, will no longer hold back your own development for the benefit of the family since you have trust in your parents' ability to reach a workable decision about the future of their relationship.

Johann could conceivably help Sylvia at present by temporarily taking on the role of a supplier of anxieties. That would make it easier for Sylvia to give up her role as princess and to experiment with types of behavior that are appropriate for her age.

Th. 1: We are curious about which of us will be proven correct in his view. Also, we are curious about who will perhaps spring some surprises and who will ensure that stability and traditions remain sufficiently represented. As a date for another joint session, we suggest . . . (six weeks later).

There were two more family sessions with intervals of six or seven weeks between them. The fourth session, scheduled about three months after the third session, was suddenly cancelled. This was done by Sylvia via a telephone call. She told us that the family situation was chaotic but that she herself was doing very well. Some time previously she had found a job in a sports and fitness center. She felt healthy and hadn't been vomiting for several months. She still hadn't started menstruating again but would certainly come to see us again, she thought, when she got back up to 112 pounds. In her estimate this would be the case in about four weeks. Our follow-up study, carried out approximately two years later, proved that she had been right in this estimate (see follow-up interview in Chapter 11).

9

Therapy After the First Interview

THE SCHEDULE

Initially the intervals between the sessions are four to six weeks; later—after the fourth or fifth encounter—we tend to lengthen the intervals, meaning that the complete course of therapy often takes more than 18 months. If after six or seven sessions, treatment has not already terminated or the end of treatment is not yet in sight, we usually remind the family that 10 is the maximum number of sessions we normally allow for. Frequently, however, a continuing link involving minor binding is helpful. So we tell families toward the end of therapy that we would like to contact them occasionally and that in one to two years' time we will be available for a followup session.

What Form Do the Sessions Following the First Interview Take?

As described in Chapter 7 the first interview has three major functions: gaining information *on* the system, input of information *into* the system, and the establishment of a sound relationship *with* the system. These functions remain operative in the following interviews but there are changes in emphasis. The input of information designed to effect change becomes more important. We use the term *intervention* to describe these input operations.

These interventions can be divided into two categories: the interventions initiated during the interviews and the final/closing intervention. Ideally these two categories are naturally supportive and attuned to each other in order to ensure maximum effectiveness. For the purposes of this book, however, we discuss them separately here.

As already demonstrated in the preceding chapters, we consider questioning to have the greatest intervention potential *during* the sessions. The questions are designed to trigger new constructions of reality and search processes remaining in effect long after the session itself. In the final intervention, by contrast, we not only ask questions but also give instructions.

What Is of Particular Note at the Beginning of the Later Interviews?

In the first interview we are guided in the choice of our questions by the feedback we receive from the family. And in the following sessions we also base our choice of interventions on the family's reaction to what has gone before, that is, to the interventions used in the preceding session. Thus, when we see the family four to six weeks later, the central question for *us* is "Has anything changed in the family or not?" Our main concern here is with changes in the status of related individuation and/or family-wide coindividuation and coevolution.

We may recall at this point that individuation in its essence involves both a demarcation process and the formulation of and adherence to aims and values that differ from those prevailing in the immediate environment. Further, individuation signifies the ability and the willingness to tolerate the tension of ambivalence, and finally the ability and willingness to assume responsibility for oneself. Hence our question about whether changes in the dynamics of individuation as described above are to be observed within the family or not. We are equally attentive here to the facts and events recounted by the family members and to the way they recount them, the way they present themselves, and how they behave toward each other.

Basically, we have two situations here. Either there are changes to be noted or there are not. We shall discuss the former situation first: changes *are* to be observed.

First, let us give a word of warning: Relevant changes may only emerge when we have done some fairly intensive probing. In other words, things that *we* see as changes by no means necessarily appear as such to the family. Indeed, what frequently happens is that things that we look upon as positive changes are either dismissed as insignificant or rejected as undesirable by the family as a whole or individual members of it. In such a case we may assume that these changes have been experienced as representing a threat, as taking place too quickly, or as posing too much of a problem, thus provoking countermeasures on the part of the family.

In many cases these countermeasures are operative on two levels at the same time. Genuine progress toward individuation is represented as banal and "nothing special," while certain unpleasant aspects are overemphasized. For example, our questions reveal that Maria (I.P.) has been shutting herself up in her own room more often, while at the same time both seeking and finding more contact with young people of her own age. The mother's comment on this is: "Maria is getting more and more unsociable, withdrawing from the family and letting other girls put silly ideas into her head." Another typical countermove is to put the focus back on the symptoms. For example, "The inconsiderate and impertinent way that Maria just takes what she wants from the refrigerator has reawakened all our old fears and is also extremely annoying." Here no mention is made of the fact that the relationship between the siblings had undergone a distinct change. They were doing more together, while at the same time having different groups of friends. Another frequent countermeasure is to query the usefulness of therapy; or again, individual members of the family or the whole group expected for a session cancel the appointment or simply fail to turn up. Occasionally other therapists or intermediaries who have been consulted notify us that they are concerned about the course that the therapy is taking or consider a different therapeutic approach (e.g., psychoanalysis) to be more appropriate.

For us, these reactions are normally indications that we have been pressing for change too rigorously and have thus overtaxed the family. In such cases it is usually advisable to temporarily revert to the nonchange angle and to actively query the value of further sessions with the family.

Another possible reaction to the first interview (and other intervention factors) is for changes in individuation dynamics to be assessed as positive and helpful by individual family members or all of them. In this case we feel it is necessary to give the credit for these changes to the family alone and to explicitly acknowledge their achievement. However, it is also necessary to add a certain amount of skepticism: "We feel this is too good to last and we would be surprised if there weren't a relapse." (On the other hand, of course, we have to convey to the family that we have confidence in their potential for further development and that we consider what they have achieved to be lasting and substantial.) It is frequently best to resort to splitting (in the team or individual therapist) to put across these apparently contradictory messages.

The second alternative is no change, even when probed for systematically. In this case we as therapists have to ask ourselves a number of questions: Are the hypotheses underlying the interventions in the first interview accurate? Was the relationship with individual members and the family as a whole sound enough for the interventions to "take"? Has our information input been too extensive and too confusing? Was the circular questioning approach perhaps not the appropriate method for this particular family? Have we overlooked people with an important relationship to the patient (e.g., a grandparent or a therapist)? Have we been inexplicit about expectations? The answers to these questions will then determine how we proceed.

Relapse Prevention

Before the break normally preceding our closing intervention, we usually pose a number of questions designed to prevent relapse. For example: "What would each of you have to do to reinforce X's (the patient's) symptomatic (problematic) behavior? What would we therapists have to do to convey to the family that further interviews are not worth conducting or are too difficult or too dangerous?" If we know from the family's past history that more or less extreme reactions are possible (including the likelihood of a drastic stepping-up of food refusal), we attempt to anticipate these. Another question we usually put to the family before this break in the interview is: "Is there anything important that has not yet been talked about that we absolutely need to know when deliberating on what we should say to the family about how things are to proceed?"

FINAL INTERVENTION

We conclude almost all our sessions with a final intervention. It represents a renewed attempt, in concentrated and systematic form, to introduce information into the system which, particularly in the time before the next session, will make a difference to the lives of the family members. The break gives us time to give this intervention ample thought and to plan its execution in minute detail. Quite frequently this final intervention has been called a "prescription," sometimes a "paradoxical prescription." But these terms are too restrictive. The final intervention may quite simply be our saying: "We have nothing to add to what we have said already and we'll be meeting again on the. . . ." Usually, however, we give a summarizing interpretation and/or set a task or tasks. The same holds true here as for other aspects of our procedure—we must avoid implicit allocations of blame, preserve neutrality, provoke or calm as the situation demands. In short, here as everywhere, it is important to find an appropriate balance between confirmation and innovation.

The final intervention is an opportunity for the team to show how creative it is. The main criterion for the choice of intervention is the assessment of the resilience of the team's relationship with the family and the extent to which a complementary or symmetrical interactional mode prevails. If the attitude toward the therapist is more complementary, then it is fairly safe to expect that recommendations will be accepted and that the tasks set will be carried out. If there is a greater tendency toward symmetrical escalation, then this can be utilized by challenging the family to prove to the therapists that they were wrong in their assessments or expectations. For example, we may say to the warring parents of a bulimic girl who have never been able to agree on anything: "About 80% of the parents we know are able, in such a difficult situation, to reach an agreement on the behavior they should display toward their daughter. In your case we have our doubts. In our view, you belong to the 20% who find it impossible." In the family therapy literature this kind of procedure is also dealt with under the heading "compliance-based versus defiance-based interventions."

Whatever form the final intervention may take, it must convince those to whom it is addressed, it must make sense and be substantiated by a good explanation which is implicit in the preceding interventions and/or is supplied together with the final intervention.

The following list of final interventions is by no means complete. We are only listing those that we have found to be helpful in connection with anorexia families.

Positive Connotation/Reinterpretation

We emphasize once again by this intervention what the index patient is doing for the whole family, siblings included—the way in which she supports family cohesion, displays loyalty, embodies a family tradition and system of values going across generational boundaries. White (1983) has described how this value system, with its code of self-denial in the service of the other family members, is taken to extremes and hence ad absurdum by the anorectic. Like White, we too have found it particularly effective to continue a matter-of-fact description or revelation of this situation, with explicit recognition of the functions performed by the anorectic daughter.

The "As-If" Prescription

This form of intervention, described in detail by Madanes (1981) and others, is particularly useful when a number of partners are trapped in a symmetrical interaction—in other words, an escalating power struggle. We prescribe the behavior that will typically aggravate the escalation but with the proviso that the behavior must only be displayed when the person concerned does not feel like being provocative but is tenderly or amicably disposed to his or her partner. The partner is told to try to determine and to write down (unnoticed by the partner concerned) when this "as-if" behavior is displayed. Even if the partners are unable to perform this task, the symmetrical pattern is usually substantially disrupted. The partners are constantly preoccupied with the question, "Is this (normally escalating) behavior genuine or phony?" And this is indeed a very different game from the one played previously. One reservation has to be made, however. Within the range of anorexia familes we have treated, we have found such "as-if" prescriptions to be most effective in bulimia families where aggressive and symmetrical behavior can be openly manifested.

Prescribing Rituals

When we feel that past losses that family members have not come to terms with are the major obstruction to coindividuation, we prescribe joint mourning processes or grief rituals, such as those described by Paul (1987). If our central aim is the separation of generations or subsystems, we may prescribe two-person relationships (also across generational boundaries). For example: one evening a week to be spent together by Maria and Christina (her sister), by Father and Mother, by Father and Maria, by Father and Christina, by Mother and Maria, and by Mother and Christina.

This prescription is an attempt to drive a small wedge into the cohesive setup of the family and at the same time to force the family members concerned to define their relationships with one another. Or we may prescribe parentification (already existing) for the children. For example: "The children should remain at home a little longer so as to make sure that their parents feel good, that there is a harmonious atmosphere in the home," and so forth. Recently, Imber-Black (1987) has made some notable suggestions for the use of rituals that are also appropriate for anorexia families. For example, she recommends that age-appropriate separations be marked by the giving of gifts in a ceremony in which the whole family takes part or that the gains and losses implicit in certain separations be noted down on certain multicolored pieces of paper which can be stored, burnt, or shared with others.

Having the Parents Tell Their Children About Their Own Separation from Their Parents

This intervention is designed to encourage both generations—parents and children—to reflect on the present separation situation, identify differences and similarities between then and now, and possibly give some thought to the things that ought to be done differently today.

A Number of Symptom-Carriers Are Contracted Together

Here we exploit the tendency of those family members who do things for others to do things for themselves (a tendency that goes right along with the family creed, as we have seen). Consider the following example. A girl who had been anorectic for a number of years was no longer dangerously thin but was still obviously underweight. Her father suffered from high blood pressure, but only took the medication prescribed if urged to do so by his wife. He was also a heavy smoker. In this case we negotiated the following contract between father and daughter: the daughter undertook to increase her weight by at least 10 pounds in the next six weeks, while the father undertook to give up smoking and to get his blood pressure under control by taking his medicine on his own and checking his condition by taking his own blood pressure regularly. The mother was instructed to make sure that both partners adhered to the contract. After six weeks the daughter had indeed gained 10 pounds and the father had given up smoking and reduced his blood pressure to the required level by taking his medication regularly.

Introduction of a Higher Power That Is Stronger than the Anorectic Patient, the Family, and the Therapists

We may say, for example, that the defiance and the pride of the patient, her loyalty to family tradition, and so forth are stronger than anything that she, her family, and we therapists can marshal against her symptomatic or problematic behavior. In such a case we might still suggest that the patient report to us at regular (one- or two-week) intervals, informing us whether and to what extent this defiance, pride, and unswerving loyalty continue to prevail.

Prescribing Bulimic Behavior in the Context of an Imagined Father Relationship

Hellinger (personal communication, 1987) reported a prescription he had successfully given to young women displaying bulimic behavior. After experience with this approach, we can confirm that these interventions make sense for these young women and are also an effective therapeutic option.

The patients are advised to imagine, when devouring huge amounts of food, that they are sitting on their father's lap, that he is feeding them with a teaspoon, and that after each spoonful they say: "I like you to feed me, Father." They are also asked to imagine that their mother is watching. They are allowed to eat as much as they want but only with a teaspoon. In developing this approach, Hellinger was working on the assumption that the young women concerned were observing a ban by the mothers on taking anything from the fathers or that the mothers were covertly communicating to them that their fathers were not giving them anything to eat. In this view the daughters' bulimic reaction is a way of saying, "If I can only take from you, Mother, and not from Father, then I shall take so much from you that it will harm me."

Our observations confirm that young women with bulimia often seem to harbor the desire to please their fathers and develop more in common with them. But the fact that they cannot fulfil this desire may, in our opinion, be bound up with a whole range of different ideas and interaction patterns. Some maintain loyalties to their mothers because they feel that the mothers need their support against a tyrannical father (real or imagined). Others avoid contact with their fathers if they feel that the fathers find them more attractive than their wives. In one of our follow-up inquiries, a mother reported an improvement in the symptomatic behavior of her daughter after she had had a number of secret meetings alone with the father.

Writing a Letter

Occasionally we replace the final intervention with a letter that we send to all the family members involved shortly after the end of the session. This normally includes those members not actually present at the session. Indeed, such a letter can be an ideal way of reaching absent family members.

An example of this procedure took place with the Bertram family, which we will discuss in rather more detail. Like many other German families, the Bertrams were uprooted by World War II and suffered separations. The family owned a factory in East Germany which was handed over to Mr. Bertram when his father died. Mr. Bertram was 26 at the time. Mr. Bertram's only sister committed suicide together with the rest of her family when the Russians marched into Germany in 1945. After the war, Mr. Bertram fled to West Germany to avoid arrest, leaving his wife and six children behind. During the period in which Mrs. Bertram was alone with the children in East Germany, the third eldest son (one year older than the I.P.) died at age seven after a tumor operation. In 1958 the second eldest son, aged 15, suffered a fatal skiing accident and his body was only found six months later. At the beginning of the Bertrams' marriage an old fortune-teller had predicted that Mr. Bertram would have an easy time of it in life whereas his wife would have a great deal of sorrow. The deaths of these two sons had a particularly profound effect on the life of the mother.

Nineteen sixty-nine was another year of trials and tribulations for the family. Mr. Bertram's mother, who lived in the same house, became more and more confused and required a great deal of care. The factory that Mr. Bertram had established in the West went into financial difficulties. In 1971 he had to sell to avoid going bankrupt. The purchaser, however, did not take over Mr. Bertram's tax debts, as agreed, and the revenue authorities confiscated the family's entire property. The parents' marriage hit a rocky patch. Mr. Bertram had an affair with another woman. This was also the time in which the daughter Anne (one year younger than the I.P.) started skipping school and developed a drug problem, thus monopolizing the parents' attention. At the same time the oldest son left home, followed shortly after by the two younger sisters. In this period the daughter Silke developed bulimic anorexia. Her behavior was above all the expression of her feeling that she was being neglected by her mother and was generally underprivileged. The mother attempted to maintain her stance of not showing Silke any more favors than before her anorexia, but guilt feelings prompted her to yield to the demands made on her, particularly as the father often sided covertly with Silke.

The family came to us for family therapy 10 years later, after two years of individual therapy with Silke had been unsuccessful and the mother's best friend and the family's pet dog had died. This was also the time in which Mrs. Bertram learned that her husband had had an affair 10 years earlier. Mrs. Bertram and Silke were still very much in a bound-up situation. Silke frequently stole things from home that her mother was particularly fond of, demanded special services of her mother, and showed jealousy because she felt that her mother was more attentive and affectionate to her sister.

We decided to write all the members of the family a letter (at the first interview only the parents and Silke had been present). In this letter we defined one of the goals of family interviews as being able to mourn joint losses together and for each member to make the decisions determining his or her own life. In this case, however, we said we thought that reaching such a goal could have disastrous effects for at least some members of the family. We wrote that it was particularly unreasonable to expect the mother to mourn all her dead and take her leave of them while they were still on her mind so much and interfered with her happiness and personal development. We went on to describe all the members of the family as feeling short-changed and embittered so that there was little hope of achieving greater unity in the framework of family sessions. Also we portrayed the family as believing, on the basis of their experiences, that disasters were more likely to occur when one feels happy and content with one's lot. Therefore, paradoxically, their best hope of preventing a catastrophe was the avoidance of happiness and contentment.

We also told the family that we could not advise them to make any decisions because their reluctance to do so was a guarantee of continuing cohesion for the family after its long history of separations and ensured that nobody felt superfluous, rejected, or isolated.

We closed the letter by stressing the value of Silke's behavior in this situation. It was her anorexia and her behaving like a headstrong little girl that had kept her mother occupied and in halfway normal psychological shape after the death of Silke's two brothers and the loss of the three other children who had moved elsewhere. The mother, we wrote, could only tolerate antagonistic closeness with another person. At the same time, Silke was keeping the parents together because of their joint concern for her health. Another valuable contribution she was making was enabling her brothers and sisters to go their own way and not to have to concern themselves with their parents too much. The only thing that we therapists could do, we concluded, was to accompany the family for a while on their different paths.

In response to our letter we received the following reply from Silke's younger sister:

Dear Sirs,

When my sister gave me your letter my first reaction was to blow my top! I took it to be the "death sentence" for us all (particularly for my sister and my parents), signed and sealed by a couple of scientists with the audacity to pass judgment after an interview lasting one single hour on the internal workings of six entirely different individuals.

Why "death sentence"? Because nobody is likely to want to go on living after they've been told that their search for happiness, love, and life (or whatever) is pointless, given that it is precisely this seeking and hoping that have, until now, represented the "meaning of life" for them.

But then I started asking myself why it should annoy me so much that two complete strangers tell me I might as well give up looking, that everything is fine as it is and I am free of guilt and anxiety since my sister is looking after that side of things for me. Now, assuming that I've understood your letter correctly, I feel that you have done an excellent job of assessing the way things are with us and have put your finger on the weak points of each one of us, or at least those you have spoken to (although of course that is much easier for you than it is for us or anyone else—you don't have to watch what you say, since you're not involved in the same way as we are).

You've held up to Silke and our parents their own behavior and the impression that this behavior conveys and attribute to them different motivations than they believe they have. This incredible provocation is probably the one and only hope of moving us from the set positions and stereotypes that we have got bogged down in. True, it's conceivable that the two people most affected—Silke and my mother—will reject your theories outright and this would be a setback. But it's also conceivable that a change will take place. For example, criticizing my mother, or rather quite simply pointing out to her that she has never mourned the deaths in our family and never taken leave of them (my parents' house is a museum!) may make for change, but it could also make her close up completely. And calling Silke a headstrong little girl supplying phony worries to keep her parents occupied must be very hard and hurtful for her. Of course, you can't know much about the rest of us, but your saying that we live entirely free of guilt feelings and have been able to discard the problems we have with our parents thanks to our family martyr is what prompted me to write you this letter.

I spoke briefly with Silke about whether there was any point in me joining in the therapy and she said she couldn't see that I had any problems. The main problem, she said, was her relationship with our parents and perhaps also our parents' relationship with one another. Now I'm not sure to what extent this statement is a function of Silke's condition, in other words whether she's afraid that if I were there I'd be taking something away from her. It seems to me that we're all equally involved, even if we don't have anorexia and our problems show themselves in other ways. I would like to take part in the therapy although I can't imagine how anything can be changed just by talking about it. As to whether the therapy as a whole, and above all Silke's, could benefit from my joining in, that is something that only you can decide. I would be grateful for a reply.

Yours sincerely.

The therapists' impression was that this letter, in addition to things that were said in the sessions, did indeed help the parents to gain greater distance from Silke and to do things together and also that Silke was generally more content (she bought a house of her own and found a congenial job); but at the same time the feeling of powerlessness and of having been singled out by fate were considered to be still highly operative in family relationships.

WHEN SHOULD THERAPY BE CONCLUDED?

Following our principle of setting things in motion rather than working them through, we conclude therapy when we observe distinct progress in related individuation or family-wide coindividuation and coevolution. This means we pay less attention to changes in the symptoms than to changes in relationships. Thus it is by no means unusual for us to end therapy before menstruation has resumed and the patient has reached a desirable weight. An important indication of incipient or attained coindividuation is the establishment of relationships with age peers where these were previously absent. Another encouraging sign for us is improvement in the relationships between siblings, the development away from sibling rivalry. We also consider it a good sign when parents separate themselves off clearly from their children by unequivocally transferring responsibility for their future lives to themselves and expressing this attitude on all levels of behavior. Generally speaking we look upon it as an improvement when symmetrical escalation is replaced by dialogue. And by dialogue we mean listening to others, acting in concert, being ready and able both to assert oneself and to back down, and to negotiate a balance between proximity and distance, rights and duties, that is appropriate to the particular situation.

We would, however, advise caution about regarding a child leaving home as an unequivocal criterion for individuation. Frequently a return home under more or less dramatic circumstances is a possibility, with the person concerned proving, sooner or later, incapable of assuming responsibility for a life of her own outside the family. Another familiar manifestation of this is spending hours on phone calls home, thus remaining in constant touch with the family. In short, we should not forget that geographical separation is not synonymous with emotional separation and individuation.

In many cases we have found it valuable to arrange a follow-up interview about a year after termination of family therapy. If it is not possible for all involved to attend, we request a written report or phone call. In this way we maintain a connection between ourselves and the family and thus facilitate the individuation process in this area as well.

SPECIAL SITUATIONS

Acute Mortality Risk

Working as we do in an outpatient institution, we have been faced with particular problems on those occasions when patients in our care were in acute danger of actually starving themselves to death. In such situations it is up to us to decide whether we are going to give up our neutral stance and have them hospitalized or take the risk and continue working with the family. If we opt for the latter course, then we leave it to the family to decide— after consulting with the specialist for internal medicine treating the girl in question—whether they are prepared to assume the responsibility for outpatient treatment or not. In a number of cases where this responsibility has been shouldered by the family one of the parents was a physician.

Here again, circular questioning is our most important intervention tool. We use it here to anticipate the death of the patient, asking, for example, who would be most deeply affected by her death, who would get over it most quickly, and so forth. We also use this technique to organize a "dry family lunch." Unlike the sessions described by Minuchin and his colleagues (1978), we do not serve an actual meal; instead we use questions to "stage" certain constellations, asking who would behave in what way if Maria decided to carry on with or even step up her hunger strike. For example: "Which of the parents, feeling that Maria's life was in danger, would be more likely to insist on her being fed even if Maria rejected this very firmly? How would the other parent then behave? Would Maria see this as proof that her parents don't intend to let her die or as proof that they respect her autonomy, which in the last resort is also the autonomy to take the decision to live or die?" In this case we feel it important to have the entire session (one-and-a-half to two hours) revolve around just this topic.

What Is to Be Done in the Case of Suicidal Behavior?

Basically, an uncompromising hunger strike is a form of suicide. Overt suicidal behaviors or threats are occasionally encountered in bulimic patients. In principle the same applies here as in the case of the long-term suicides represented by extreme anorectics. We use circular questioning to investigate what these potential suicide attempts signify, to whom they are directed, and how the family members would react if the suicide succeeded.

Sudden Phone Calls and Coalition Offers

In the intervals between sessions we regularly receive urgent phone calls from some member of the family asking for advice or offering to tell us a secret. Such offers of secret collusion or coalition are refused politely but firmly. Very rarely do we let ourselves be persuaded to bring forward the date of the next appointment. Normally it helps to refer explicitly to the closing intervention of the last session and to relate the caller's behavior to it. Here, as in other cases where the therapist is confronted with unexpected situations, the cotherapist is very often a great help. He or she functions as a discussion partner in the attempt to clarify the situation and to establish or reestablish a meta-perspective. He or she can also be called upon if the closing intervention involves splitting, that is, the therapists taking different positions. In this constellation the cotherapist makes it easier to mirror the family's own ambivalence and thus helps them to accept it more easily; if this fails to work, then the one side of this ambivalence (in the form of an expectation, an idealization, possibly also a projection) sometimes remains directed at the therapist. In general, however, we make less use of splitting in our treatment of anorexia families than we do with families with schizophrenic or manic-depressive members.

10

A Course of
Family Therapy

We devoted much of Chapter 1 to the Landmanns and also went into some detail about what we learned in the course of the sessions with them. We now summarize the process of these sessions, focusing here on the closing interventions.

Over a period of 14 months, we conducted 12 interviews with this family. Two therapists took active part in the sessions, with one and sometimes two colleagues behind the one-way mirror. All interviews were recorded on tape or on video cassettes.

THE FIRST INTERVIEW

Here the parents and the two daughters took part. Both parents give the impression of being rather older than they actually are. Mr. Landmann is of medium height, wears a suit, uses a formal civil-servant type language, and proves approachable and demonstratively polite. Mrs. Landmann, slim, pale and carefully dressed, displays the outward features of a hard-working and self-sacrificing wife and mother. She constantly attempts to harmonize and only participates in the proceedings if she is openly criticized or feels that her principles are being called into question. Jutta (age 22) is also very slim and gives the impression of being cool, matter-of-fact, and detached in her attitude. Petra (age 19) wears loose-fitting clothes that conceal the contours of her body. She is very thin (70 pounds) and is the one most likely to betray her feelings (sometimes abruptly). She also gives us most of the relevant information on the relationships between the members of her family. Shortly before this first interview she had returned home after an unsuccessful nine-month period in a psychiatric ward for children and adolescents.

We ask very few questions about symptoms and these are not explicitly offered for discussion. The main topics of the interview are the relationships of the family members with one another (including the two grandmothers who are both in need of care), the distribution of roles, the handling of feelings (particularly anger and annoyance), and the negative attitude shown by the whole family. This attitude and the system of values underlying it will be concerning us for a number of sessions to come. In this first interview we also learn something about the parents' families of origin (see Chapter 1).

Our closing commentary basically consists of a positive association to the behavior displayed by the whole family and a specific request to Petra.

We acknowledge the parents' readiness to put their own interests second to those of others. Mrs. Landmann, we say, has largely given up having any life of her own so as to be able to care for other members of the family (particularly the grandmothers and Petra). Mr. Landmann we describe as having forgone a more intimate relationship with his wife because he has intuitively realized how important it is to his wife to be there for others. Jutta we present as doing without friendships in order to gain recognition in her work and thus enhance the family's status. Petra is described as helping her in this by functioning as a source of worry. By keeping her parents concerned about her she reduces tension between them and also ensures that they have more common ground. This keeps the father from going his own way more often than he does.

Petra reveals in the course of the interview that she is looking for a small apartment of her own. We ask her to stay at home until she is sure that her mother no longer needs anyone to look after and has found other things to live for. In doing so, we say, she is making a laudable sacrifice in the interests of the family.

This summing up provokes a variety of reactions. Jutta immediately confirms that Petra's illness has consolidated her parents' relationship and given them more common ground. Petra says she feels sure that her parents consider what the therapists have said to be utter nonsense. The parents deny this immediately. Mr. Landmann also rejects the claim that he has ever had a tendency to go his own way, and this prompts Petra to remind him that there was an occasion when he had considered leaving the family to live elsewhere. When the therapists ask Petra to stay home for the time being she starts to cry bitterly, saying that she couldn't take it any longer. She leaves the room in a violent temper and her outbursts are audible all the way down the stairs. The parents leave in embarrassment.

SECOND INTERVIEW (NINE WEEKS LATER)

Petra has now taken an apartment of her own in the same town and has also spent a weekend visiting Jutta in Cologne. A great deal of the session revolves around the sisters' relationship and Jutta's do-or-die independence and her lack of contacts outside the family. It becomes obvious that there is strong rivalry between the two sisters. Other topics broached are the marked tendency toward self-sacrifice displayed by all the women, and the subject of happiness in life (existent and nonexistent) and giving and taking. Asked about their image of women, the female members of the family reveal that they experience men as impulsive, uncontrolled, and sexually aggressive. Petra's language in particular is marked by strong sexual symbolism. In our closing commentary after the break, we emphasize the competition between the women members of the family as to who is best at self-sacrifice. We then ask whether the women will be more likely to succeed in getting Mr. Landmann to be more self-sacrificing or whether Mr. Landmann will manage to convince his wife and daughters to enjoy life more. We predict that the latter case is more likely and that in the long run Mr. Landmann will develop guilt feelings if he continues to be the only one to indulge himself occasionally. This will then finally lead him to a self-sacrificing stance as well.

THIRD INTERVIEW (FOUR WEEKS LATER)

Petra has returned home, saying she felt too lonely in her apartment. Her eating problems have been aggravated by this loneliness. However, the family emphasize that in the last interview things had been discussed that they have never previously been able to talk about within the family. When we come back to our closing commentary at the previous session, a large number of facts and events are described which confirm the escalation of the martyr game in this family. Only the father continues to reject this version with regard to himself: "Self-sacrifice has never been an ideal of mine." Petra says: "If you don't get anything for a long time, then you have nothing to give either." We then pose the hypothetical question about what would happen if over a long period the individual members were no longer given or refused to accept anything. The mother would become even more embittered and careworn, but as long as the father took her side she would not fall ill. When we asked which members of the (extended) family are most likely to indulge themselves from time to time, we hear rather disparaging accounts of the irresponsibility and happy-go-lucky attitudes of some of them.

Closing Commentary in Third Interview

We emphasize that we probably came across to the family as being too intent on promoting Petra's moving out of the house. We acknowledge that Petra, by returning home, has shown her ability to learn from experience and to care for herself. We consider it our task during the next sessions to watch out that things do not change prematurely.

FOURTH INTERVIEW (SIX WEEKS LATER, WITHOUT JUTTA)

Petra's condition and eating behavior are unchanged. Mr. Landmann says: "The vision of us all standing at Petra's graveside overwhelms us and keeps on appearing." We use question techniques to anticipate Petra's death and also ask about possible reactions if the grandmothers die. We hear at length about the circumstances in which the child they lost died. When the atmosphere becomes increasingly tense and the mother in particular expresses doubts about the value of continuing with family sessions, we change the subject. We learn that things always tend to come to a head when Father, Mother, and Petra are together. Mr. Landmann says: "I feel that Petra's general condition would improve if her relationship with her mother were better." Petra responds: "Rubbish. Improvement of the general condition!" Father reacts: "Petra, that's the whole problem, that's the key to it all!" Petra says *(loudly)*: "I'm a person and not just the improvement of a general condition!" Father: "But we want you to be a person again, happy and contented." Petra: "I can't go on!" *(sobs)*.

When we ask whether tensions have eased or increased recently, we hear that, if anything, they have increased.

Prescription After the Break

We tell the family that we feel we have dwelt too much on the separations and deaths in the family's past. This is too much for the family and makes for increased tension, and it is not a good idea to go on talking about this subject. We also report, however, that our colleague behind the one-way mirror is struck by the fact that Petra's behavior is reminiscent of Gabile (the child who died in early infancy), who was also very thin and had to be force-fed.

We say that one thing we feel to be vital, however, is that Gabile should finally be given a proper place to rest and a symbolic funeral. The family is asked to get together before the next interview and to compose the inscription for a gravestone for

Gabile. We request the members of the family to keep out of each other's way more in the weeks to come and warn Petra not to act on her plans for moving to Cologne too soon.

FIFTH INTERVIEW (EIGHT WEEKS LATER)

The family has agreed on a gravestone inscription for the dead child; it is "Our Gabile" and the dates of her birth and her death. The mother emphasizes immediately that this is the end of the matter, and Petra is very much against having a gravestone actually put up. She says she will feel as if she is being buried as well. Jutta's reaction is: "She's afraid of a gravestone being put up with space on it for her name."

Taken altogether, however, the family appears emotionally more accessible and able to listen to one another with greater composure. The parents tell us how much of a strain it was for them to decide on the question of life-prolonging measures for their fathers when they were dying. At the end of the interview all the members of the family express to Petra their desire that she should live and Petra emphasizes that she intends to make sure that she stays alive. The therapists' impression is that something new is happening in the family. They conclude the interview without a closing commentary, merely saying that they have nothing to add to what has been communicated during the session.

SIXTH INTERVIEW (ONE WEEK LATER)

Because we need a family for a live supervision session in a seminar with Gianfranco Cecchin and Luigi Boscolo, we ask the Landmanns if they are willing to participate and they are agreeable. In the preliminary talk-through we decide that the therapists should pay particular attention to the period of the onset of symptoms (three-and-a-half years earlier). It becomes apparent that Petra felt neglected by her mother after the death of her grandfather, the reason being that after Jutta left home her mother turned to Jutta more and took her into her confidence. At the end of the supervision, we ask a number of questions about the

future. We ask the family to come back the next day and we
work out the following prescription together, which Dr. Boscolo
is to communicate to the family on the following day:

In the meantime we have discussed yesterday's session and
have asked the therapists to request you to return today
because the situation has taken a dramatic turn. It is dramatic
because Petra has lost so much weight. If she loses a few
pounds more, she may well die.

From what we witnessed yesterday and from our experience with other families, we can say that we are very
impressed by the deep, positive bond existing between Petra
and her mother and the mother and Petra.

We understand, Mrs. Landmann, that Petra was born after
you had lost two other babies. The effect of this was to
make the bond from Petra to Mother and Mother to Petra
very close. As I just said, we are convinced of the strong
positive bond between Mother and Petra and Petra and
Mother. In the last few years, however, the relationships
between Petra and Mother and Mother and Petra have
deteriorated. They are not as good as they were and we
have asked ourselves why. We know from experience that
particularly when a daughter decides to stop eating, the
positive feelings between daughter and mother and mother
and daughter cease. Because the mother is worried about
her daughter not eating she tries to persuade her to eat and
because the mother gets worked up the daughter stops eating.
And your relationship has worsened in this way too. We
have asked ourselves why Mother and Petra and Petra and
Mother stopped showing each other their positive feelings
at a certain point. We believe—from experience we have of
other cases—that they have decided not to display their
positive feelings for one another and not to express their
profound love for one another as a way of conveying to
other members of the family that there is no need for them
to feel excluded. In the present case Jutta would feel excluded,
as would Father and in particular the grandmothers, who
have lost their husbands in recent years and are now very
largely dependent on the mother.

So both Mother and Petra have loosened their bond with each other so that nobody—neither Jutta nor Father, and especially not the grandmothers—need feel left out. But we feel that they have gone too far in this sacrificing of their good relationship, their deep, positive bond.

It is for this reason, and because the situation is so dramatic, that we have asked you to come back here today. We believe that it is very important for Mother and Petra and Petra and Mother to have one day a week to to themselves in the coming months and that Father, Jutta, and the grandmothers should accept this Petra-Mother/Mother-Petra day.

What we see is that Mother and Petra and Petra and Mother have been the ones to suffer most in the last few years because they have realized that Father, Jutta, and the grandmothers were being excluded. In this situation we feel that it is very important for Petra and Mother and Mother and Petra to have one day in the week to be on their own together. The two of them alone will decide what they are going to do on this one day a week. They can either be side by side, talk to each other, be silent together, fight each other, or treat each other lovingly, just how they happen to feel on that particular day. The other members of the family should keep away and make this day possible for them.

It is necessary and important for Petra and Mother and Mother and Petra not to inform anybody of what they have been doing together on that particular day, and the other members of the family should refrain from asking how Petra and Mother and Mother and Petra have spent that day together. When Father and Mother get home after this interview, they should tell the grandmothers that someone else will be looking after them on this particular day of the week—perhaps Jutta, when she's there, or a babysitter or a nurse, always on Petra-Mother/Mother-Petra days.

Dr. Boscolo then inquires about days that would suit both of them. Petra is violently against the idea because the parents had planned going on vacation for the next 14 days. The parents are willing to extend their sacrifices to this vacation too. Finally, there is agreement that this Petra-Mother/Mother-Petra day should start immediately after the parents' return from their vacation:

If you feel tempted to spend more than one day a week alone together, you should still not give in to this temptation. We feel it could be dangerous for the rest of the family, particularly the grandmothers, who are so dependent on the mother. If Petra loses more weight it may be best to put her in hospital. We have a great deal of experience with these problems and do not believe that hospitalization helps to solve them. But if it does prove necessary, the mother should go to the hospital on the day to be spent together and stay there with Petra the whole day. You should not now discuss what we have prescribed because Mother and Petra and Petra and Mother will only be starting with their days when the parents get back from their vacation.

SEVENTH INTERVIEW (FIVE WEEKS LATER)

The parents have been on vacation together and have had a good time. At the end of the vacation they had wanted to spend a few days with Petra but Petra refused. In the meantime, Petra and her mother have spent the day together on three occasions. For the mother it was very difficult not to tell her husband where they were staying or going, since it had been usual in the family for the last 30 years for everybody to know where the others were. Petra had brought back souvenirs for her father from these excursions, thus telling him indirectly where they had been. Mrs. Landmann is very taken with this attentiveness on Petra's part, saying how good it was for everyone to have a share in such things: "It shows that we belong together, doesn't it?" The father found it strange that the family should not be allowed to talk about Petra and Mother's joint outings.

While Father and Jutta feel that things are deteriorating and complain of the hostile atmosphere within the family, Mother and Petra insist that things have gotten better. Petra says: "I can tell from my pants. They're tighter."

Closing Commentary After the Break

We tell the family that the team is divided in its opinion. Whereas one of us has the impression that there is little change, a colleague behind the one-way mirror says that Jutta is obviously doing worse while Petra is obviously a great deal better. He has expressed the fear that Jutta could take a further turn for the worse if Petra and Mother continued to get on better. His suggestion is that in the next few weeks Mother and Petra ought not to let the others notice if they continue to do better.

We report that our Italian colleagues had predicted that it would be very difficult for Mother and Petra to perform the task as prescribed and had recommended setting the same task in a less extreme form if it should turn out to be too difficult for them. In the next few weeks, Petra and Mother and Mother and Petra should only spend five or six hours together on their one day a week. However, our colleagues had, we said, asked us to tell the family that the most important thing was for the time spent together to be on the same day every week. As this was likely to be a particularly difficult period for Jutta—Father would probably be better able to come to terms with the situation—we arrange a meeting before Christmas when Jutta is also back home again.

EIGHTH INTERVIEW (SIX WEEKS LATER)

In this session the family displays obvious changes. All the members appear calmer, more content, and more cheerful. Jutta has brought her boyfriend home with her. There is extensive discussion of the daughters' relationships with men. In the interim Mr. and Mrs. Landmann have frequently been out together on their own.

Closing Commentary

We show our surprise at the positive changes. We cannot find any really satisfactory explanation for them. But we say that it seems that Petra has found the ideal solution in this situation. As her mother is at present under very great strain looking after the grandmothers, Petra causes her mother fewer worries while at the same time ensuring with her very low weight that there is no danger of a man finding her attractive. We ask Jutta not to talk to Petra too much about her boyfriend as it is too early for Petra to get involved with relationships of that kind. Mrs. Landmann is given another task, namely to do more in the coming weeks to alleviate her husband's stress and tension.

When we openly query the value of family sessions and consider discontinuing them, the family insists on being given a new appointment.

NINTH INTERVIEW (EIGHT WEEKS LATER)

The family is still improving. Petra looks well and we are told that she has been seeing a lot of people her own age. She complains, however, that her new-found frankness and openness are often not responded to. Her grandmother is now defined as the family's major problem. Conflicts are expressed more openly. The discussion centers mainly on attention, recognition, tenderness, and the future.

Closing Commentary

We tell the family that we fear that Petra is improving too rapidly and prescribe her a relapse. Her mother in particular, we say, needs her for a while longer, finding it easier to confide in her and take comfort from her than her husband. Petra's reaction is: "I'm damned if I'm going to lose weight again!" We also communicate that we find it difficult to say why in this family, unlike others, the daughters had not developed mutual solidarity and support in their progress toward independence. To improve our understanding of this we say that we would like to see the daughters alone at the next-but-one interview. We then tell them that we see it as our task to slow down the improvement somewhat, and for this reason intend to prolong the intervals between sessions.

TENTH INTERVIEW (EIGHT WEEKS LATER)

In this interview the main topics are the relationships of the parents with each other as well as those of the sisters. The generational boundary between parents and daughters seems to the therapists to be more strongly marked.

There is no closing commentary.

ELEVENTH INTERVIEW (EIGHT WEEKS LATER)

As agreed, only the daughters come to this session. We quickly bring the discussion round to the rivalry between them. Both feel that the basis for it lies in the fact that the parents had always portrayed each to the other as exemplary. The therapists concentrate more on Jutta's attempts at self-definition and her performance-oriented attitude. Petra tells us that a friend of the family has been heard to say that the mother is depressed at the moment because Petra has more interest in life and so the mother no longer has control over her and can no longer keep her for herself. This friend went on to say that the mother should be glad and that it was better to have a healthy, cheerful daughter outside the home than a walking corpse at home. Petra, however, also shows understanding for the parents, not finding it easy to come to terms with her changeable moods and sometimes irritable behavior. For her mother, she says, it's either "there forever" or "gone forever" and nothing in between, and reports her as saying: "I've worried myself sick about you for five years and now I'm through with letting myself be worn down to the ground!" Petra is convinced that her anorexia is a thing of the past. When she gets her period again, she says, she'll be celebrating with champagne.

Closing Commentary

We acknowledge the surprising positive changes and the tact and sensitivity shown to each other by the sisters during the session. But we also communicate our impression that the parents are not doing so well. While it would be unfair to oblige Petra to help her parents by taking a turn for the worse, we say that we don't think it would be right to put all the strain on Jutta and have her solely responsible for the parents' well-being because we feel that at the moment she is not doing as well as Petra. We therefore set the daughters the task of taking weekly turns at being responsible for the parents, adding that this task might help the whole family to learn that there is not only the "here for good" or "gone for good" but also such a thing as a flexible combination of self-definition and being-there-for-others. The daughters are asked not to tell the parents about this task. Finally we also tell them that we are not sure whether the sisters might have gotten too close to one another during the session; in any event, they should not pursue getting closer to each other in the immediate future because if they get too close then one of them will have to make a major effort to separate herself off again.

TWELFTH INTERVIEW (EIGHT WEEKS LATER)

We see the parents without their daughters. They say that they are less worried; even though Petra's symptoms have not disappeared completely, she is a great deal more approachable and is even heard to laugh from time to time. The mother says her main worry is when Petra stays away overnight without telling anyone when she intends coming home. With questions about the future, we address the question of the parents' relationship when both daughters have gained complete independence.

Closing Commentary

We acknowledge the parents' efforts. Certainly, we would hold further sessions but we have decided to terminate the sessions with this meeting as we are now confident that the parents will be able to develop other interests in life apart from worrying and also to reorganize their relationship when their daughters leave them for good.

We thus terminated the interviews at a time when Petra still displayed obvious symptoms such as occasional vomiting and absence of menstruation. Despite this, we had the impression that the individuation and separation process within the family was

now under way and that the generations were now more clearly
defined.

FOLLOW-UP INQUIRY

Eight months after termination of the family sessions we called
to inquire for the first time how things had been going. The
mother told us that Petra was abroad and had been there for
some weeks already. She had gained weight but had not yet
started joining the family for meals. She still hadn't got her period.
There had been no medical or psychotherapeutic treatment since
the termination of therapy with us. Jutta was described as being
satisfied with her trainee post and having relationships with people
her own age. The parents were doing well.

Two years and two months later we asked a colleague to call
the family. He spoke to Petra and her mother. Petra told him
that she still had eating problems (bouts of overeating and vomiting). She now weighed 94 pounds. She had few friends and
she was still living with her parents. Family relationships were
sometimes good, sometimes bad. She frequently felt hemmed in.
She described her relationship with her sister as good ("bosom
pals"). Parents and daughters were still very much bound up
with one another, but their relationships were ambivalent.

The mother reported that Petra's eating habits were anything
but normal; she had not, however, had a geniune relapse in the
interim. She was now training to be a technical assistant with a
pharmaceutical company. Her mother found that Petra still had
problems in developing friendships; otherwise relationships in the
family were described as very close and very good. Everyone in
the family had been very upset by the death of the maternal
grandmother. Altogether, however, the mother said the situation
was incomparably better then it had been and the family sessions
had helped greatly.

11

Lessons from a Follow-up Study

In 1984 and 1987 we carried out follow-up studies on most of the anorexia families we had been treating. The first time we included 31, the second time 62 families. The findings from the first study have already been published (Stierlin & Weber, 1987).

With each study we had different aims in mind and employed different methods. Before we focus on these, we would like to comment briefly on the value and limits of outcome studies in general.

These studies provide information on the natural course of an illness or disturbance and on the efficacy of therapeutic measures. Therefore, it should not surprise us that there now exist over 50 studies, worldwide, which examine the course of anorexia nervosa after various types of therapy. Recently Hsu (1987) gave a critical overview of such studies. When compared with other outcome studies in the psychotherapeutic domain, studies of anorectics promise relatively clear-cut results. They can measure not only "soft" psychosocial factors but also "hard" data such as weight

This chapter was written in collaboration with Arnold Retzer.

gain, menstruation, and observable changes in eating behaviors. However, even here a number of methodological problems remain which have been insufficiently addressed by the existing studies. For example, Hsu (1987) mentions several serious methodological failings of outcome studies in anorexia nervosa. He mentions in particular:

- lack of clinical data and inadequate diagnostic criteria
- lack of adequate description of treatment
- inadequate follow-up (e.g., short duration of follow-up, a high failure-to-trace rate, indirect methods of evaluation, poorly defined outcome criteria, failure to employ multiple outcome measures)

We may add to this list another failing. The health of the other family members and the development of the whole family are not given enough attention. Our experience as family therapists has taught us that frequently another member develops symptoms when the symptom bearer gives up his or her symptom. We believe such family criteria have been given too little attention in the follow-up studies of anorexia families carried out so far, which is one more reason to include them in our study.

Despite the fact that family therapy is being recommended frequently for anorexia nervosa, there are only a few follow-up studies on anorectic patients treated in this modality. The best known is the study by Rosman and colleagues (1977), who belong to the team of Minuchin. However, their follow-up period is relatively short (mean = one year), with a mean length of symptoms of six months. Another follow-up study planned by Rosman and colleagues is yet to appear.

We can well understand the difficulties these authors may have had with such a study. In a study that tries to take account of the above-mentioned family factors, the methodological difficulties increase almost exponentially. And this is especially the case when one tries to establish connections between the original therapy and the improvement observed later.

As family therapists we are particularly aware of the multiple interconnections, recursive influences, and interactions occurring in living systems. That hinders our expectation that an observed change A can be attributed to a family therapy B in a monocausal and linear way.

We are further aware—and we have mentioned this already—that as therapists/observers we are always part and parcel of the results of our observations. Thus, our data appear contaminated from the very beginning. Also, we need to remind ourselves of Maturana and Varela's (1987) dictum that objectivity has to be put in parenthesis, which means that such "objectivity" is (also) created by the distinctions and the choices an observer or examiner makes. We cannot help but deal with data that have been taken out of their context and whose statistical computation suggests an objectivity that cannot be genuine.

However, the greatest difficulty may well have to do with the kind of therapy we practice. As mentioned earlier, this happens to be a therapy limited to relatively few sessions. This therapy tries to trigger changes but is not intended to work through a problem in depth (whatever that may mean). For such therapy to "take," a propitious moment in time may be necessary. After all, we see our families at a time in the individual's and family's life cycle where pressures for change or, perhaps more accurately, pressures to undergo coindividuation and coevolution, abound. Therefore, we need to ask ourselves, can we, in spite of such pressures for change and the above-mentioned difficulties, still gain some insight into how our family interviews may have impacted the members? We would like to invite the reader to consider the following in the light of this central question.

THE THEORETICAL BACKGROUND

The families to be reported on were treated during the period from 1978 until the end of 1987. For us, this was a decade of transition and new orientations. For the most part we treated seriously disturbed families. In many of them, psychoses or severe psychosomatic illnesses had been diagnosed. It was mainly our experience with these families that caused us to abstain from using the encounter model of family therapy—we have described it elsewhere (Stierlin et al., 1980)—and instead to adopt the systemic approach which we have described in the preceding chapters. A further reason for doing so was our deepening contact with the Milan group. Boscolo and Cecchin proved especially stimulating. They were the ones who helped us to turn the circular questioning approach described earlier into a kind of all-purpose instrument. They were also influential in our reducing the average number of sessions and increasing the intervals between sessions (see also Selvini Palazzoli, 1980). Whereas initially we held 15–30 sessions with rather short intervals between them, nowadays we carry through an average of 4–10 sessions with intervals from four weeks' to three months' duration.

THE FAMILIES SEEN BY US

In the decade under study we treated at our institute 70 families in which we had diagnosed an identified patient with anorexia nervosa. We include 11 other families who were treated at the Institute for Systemic Therapy and Transactional Analysis, with which one of us (G.W.) is affiliated. Of these 81 families, only four had anorectic sons. Since we gained the impression that these families differed from those with anorectic daughters in essential respects, we did not include them in our follow-up studies. In the case of five of the female patients, the earlier diagnosis of anorexia nervosa could not be confirmed beyond doubt when the criteria established by Feighner and colleagues in 1972 and by Garfinkel and Garner in 1982 were applied. Today we would diagnose two of these patients as bulimics. Three more families were excluded by the psychologist conducting the statistical analysis because the original data were insufficient. We also excluded a further seven families whose treatment began after May 1987. Thus there remained a sample of 62 families.

We included subsequently in our statistical study those 42 families who finished their family therapy at least 24 months before the latest follow-up date. Of these 42 families, 31 form the cohort of our already published study. These 31 families were contacted in 1984 by a neutral observer. This was done by way of telephone conversations. These families and 11 additional ones were recontacted in 1987. It was thus possible to check earlier statements and to let ourselves be guided by existing data.

Approximately half of the families came from the wider Heidelberg area. More than a quarter lived 200 or more kilometers away. The anorexia families under study can hardly be called a representative sample. At our institute we accept only families who either want family therapy or have been advised to try it. These are, according to our experience, for the most part strongly bound-up systems (or families with centripetal orientations).

When we did a check on our first family interviews as to whether centripetal vs. centrifugal orientations (according to the criteria established by Kelsey-Smith and Beavers in 1981) predominated, we assessed the situation as follows:

In 20 families (47.6%) we found massive family-wide centripetal orientations and in a further seven families (16.7%) centripetal tendencies that were less marked but still distinct. In 10 families we observed centripetal as well as centrifugal tendencies and only in two families did we find a predominance of family-wide centrifugal tendencies. Thus, our assumption was confirmed that it is usually strongly bound-up families who find their way to our institute. We suspect that families with younger anorectic daughters between the ages of approximately 10–13 are more frequently referred to outpatient services of departments of child and adolescent psychiatry or to pediatric clinics. Since we have relatively few therapists work at our institute, we have had to refer many families to other services. If we take the father's occupation as a rough index for the family's socioeconomic status, we find that almost 80% of our families belong either to the lower-middle class (40.5%) or to the upper-middle class (38.1%).

SOME DATA ON OUR ANORECTIC PATIENTS

At the beginning of therapy about two-thirds of our patients were either high school (25) or university students (7). All 42 were either receiving schooling or were holding jobs. At the time of the follow-up, almost three-quarters (31) of them were university students (18) or held an academic post (13).

With respect to their religion, the patients did not significantly differ from the average German population.

The parents' age at the time of the identified patient's birth appeared to us relatively high (the father's mean age was 32 years, 7 months; the mother's 28 years, 10 months). A similar finding has been reported by other authors. Garfinkel and Garner (1982) and Hall and colleagues (1986) see this as evidence of the parents' relatively high socioeconomic status. But it could also mean that these parents were or are relatively strongly bound up with their families of origin and that they were able to separate from these only haltingly and incompletely.

These families had an average of 2.46 children. In 20 out of 42 families (47.6%) the anorectic girl had a sister (15 = 35.7%) or a brother (5 = 11.9%). If we take into account only the 36 families with two or more children, we find that the anorectic girl was in 14 cases (38.9%) the oldest and in 15 cases (41.7%) the youngest child.

We were also interested to learn whether and how strongly our anorectic patients had a rivalrous relationship with a sibling. In checking our first interviews we found out that in 34 out of 42 cases our patients had a considerable or even strong competitive relationship with siblings (almost exclusively sisters) or girlfriends. Of course, one can argue that rivalry is a natural part of any sibling relationship. However, in 14 of our cases (33%) the sibling rivalry struck us as being extreme; and in two further cases we found a similarly strong rivalry in the relationship with an important girlfriend.

THE TRIGGERING SITUATION

What is viewed to be the triggering situation depends greatly on the observer's theoretical position. For example, a psychoanalyst views other factors to be relevant than a biologically oriented psychiatrist. The systemic therapist, on the other hand, tends to see changes in relationships as important. In all cases we deal more with explanations that try to make sense than with "real" causes.

We were primarily interested in what the family members (and referring therapists) had regarded as relevant in triggering anorectic behaviors. In order to get to know their opinions we asked questions such as, "And what explanation do you have for the fact that X (identified patient) has tried to starve herself at this particular point in time?" We assigned the answers and descriptions to eight areas, which we then subdivided further. Altogether 123 triggering factors (i.e., a mean of 2.9 per person) were mentioned. The eight areas and respective distribution of answers were as follows:

1. actual or feared separations in the context of the family of origin (36 = 29.37%)
2. loss of contact with peers (18 = 14.63%)
3. experiences of being slighted
4. abrupt efforts at boundary setting vis-à-vis a parent who is seen as overprotective and/or dominating (10 = 8.3%)
5. experiences, at the center of which were weight and one's figure (e.g., being teased for being too fat) (12 = 9.76%)
6. attempted avoidance of growing up and becoming a woman (8 = 6.50%)
7. attempts to attract attention and gain importance by means of anorectic behaviors (11 = 9.4%)
8. strong tensions in family relationships (15 = 12.20%)

Thus various types of situations in which separations were either taking place or threatening were most frequently mentioned. Often these centered around the serious illness or death of a close relative. In 10 cases this happened to be the death or serious illness of a grandparent. On five occasions leaving home (e.g., because of studies in another town or foreign country) was given as a major reason, and on four occasions the separation of a brother or sister from the parental home.

The answers in this list point to the special significance which the anorectic girl's ambivalent relationship with her mother seems to have. In area No. 4 there is six times mention of struggles to set oneself apart from the mother but only two times to do so with regard to the father. In area No. 7 there were 11 listings and 10 of these viewed the anorectic behavior as an attempt to elicit more attention and love from the mother. Also, in area No. 5 the mother was mentioned four times. She was the one who had attempted to reduce *her* weight about the time when her daughter started to develop anorectic symptoms.

The answers in area No. 3 suggest that sibling rivalry could be another important factor: out of 13 listings 12 carried the assumption that the patient felt slighted and disfavored as compared to a sibling. Finally, in 10 out of 15 instances there was mention of increasing tensions in the parental relationship as an important factor (area No. 8). We were surprised to find that fear of growing up and of sexuality were mentioned only rarely. This holds true for the family interviews as well as for the follow-up conversations.

Often we saw a confluence of several chains of events and causes. For example, on the one hand one could view as important actual or impending separations and losses within the family and on the other the loss of contacts with peers. We thus get the impression of mutually reinforcing circular processes. In them, different punctuations of causal pathways seem possible. For example, a girl might react with anorectic behavior when, on the one hand, the death of a grandparent increases tensions and insecurities within the family and, on the other, contacts with friends break off for one reason or another. Or again, she retreats from her peer group because the grandparent's death has created an alarming situation at home; however, back in the family fold she feels constricted and controlled. Or again, she experiences in her peer relationships a disappointment, feels simultaneously overtaxed, and therefore encapsulates herself and tries to stabilize her sense of self-worth by increasing self-control, self-punishment, and efforts to achieve.

THE PATIENTS' SYMPTOMS

All patients showed markedly dysfunctional eating behaviors. Twenty-three out of 42 (54.8%) reported vomiting; in four of these cases the anorectic behavior had clearly turned into bulimic behavior. Compared to similar studies, we found the percentage of girls who reported vomiting to be unusually high. This may be simply a characteristic of our sample but it is also conceivable that vomiting is today more easily talked about and less shamefully hidden than in earlier times.

Concerning weight, we shall omit here any correlations between age, weight, and height. Thirty-six of our patients (85.7%) weighed less than 45 kilograms (99 pounds) at the beginning of therapy, 11 of them (26.1%) less than 35 kilograms (77 pounds). Thirty-eight of 42 girls (90.5%) showed a minimal weight of less than 40 kilograms (88 pounds). The average minimal weight was 34.25 kilograms (75.35 pounds), the mean weight at the beginning of therapy 39.9 kilograms (87.80 pounds).

The mean age at the first appearance of symptoms was 14 years and 11 months. Nearly two-thirds of the girls were between 14 and 18 years old when their symptoms started. The mean age at the beginning of therapy was 18 years and two months. This means there was an average interval of three years and three months between the beginning of symptoms and the beginning of family interviews. This figure, however, may give a somewhat distorted impression. Twenty-six out of 42 patients (61.9%) entered family interviews within 24 months after the first appearance of symptoms (for exact figures see Figures 1 and 2).

Only two out of 42 patients had never been treated before entering family therapy, 27 (64.3%) had had previous outpatient therapy, and 23 (55.8%) one or more previous inpatient treatments.

FAMILY THERAPIES AND PERIOD OF FOLLOW-UP

As already mentioned, we conduct at our institute only a limited number of sessions with any given family. Forty-one out of 42 families were seen in no more than 14 sessions. On the average, there were six sessions per family (see Figure 3).

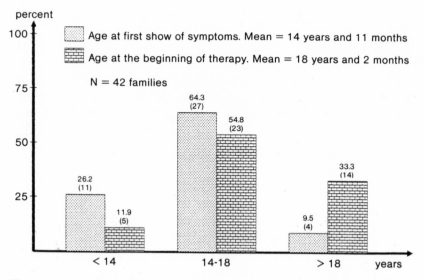

Figure 1. Age at first show of symptoms and at the beginning of family therapy.

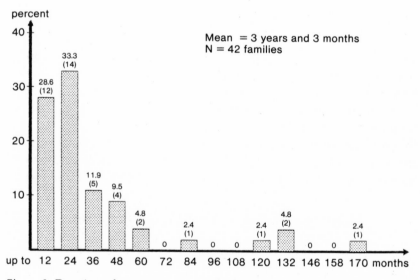

Figure 2. Duration of symptoms up to the beginning of family therapy.

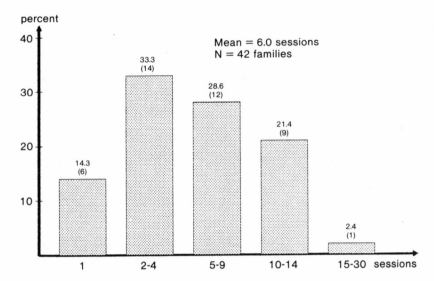

Figure 3. Number of sessions.

In more than three-quarters of the cases, the family therapy lasted less than 12 months, while the average family therapy lasted 8.7 months (see Figure 4).

All 42 families were seen by experienced therapists. In at least 30 of them (72.8%), at least one of the two authors was involved as therapist. All families except two were seen in cotherapy by two therapists. In 15 cases one or two team members served as observers behind the one-way mirror.

As already mentioned, we included in our follow-up study all families whose treatment had stopped at least 24 months prior to the follow-up date. The average follow-up period stretching from the end of the family sessions to the time of follow-up interview was four years and five months (see Figure 5).

METHODS USED IN THE FOLLOW-UP

We refer in the following to two follow-up studies: one conducted in 1984 with 31 patients and the other conducted in 1987 with 42 patients. The patients of the 1984 study were also included

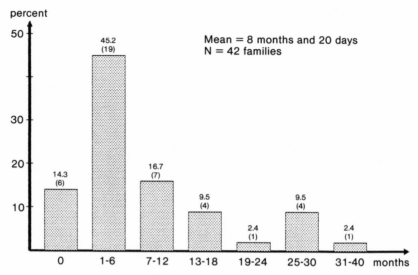

Figure 4. Duration of family therapy.

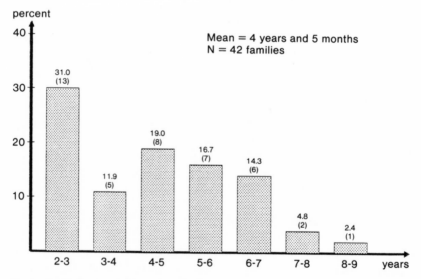

Figure 5. Maximum follow-up period.

in the 1987 study, that is, they were followed up twice. We followed up another 20 patients, bringing the total of all followed-up patients to 62, but did not include these in our detailed statistical analysis. Accordingly, we are dealing in the following with two studies with partly overlapping cohorts, the one involving 31, the other 42 patients.

The first study relied exclusively on telephone interviews. A younger colleague who had recently entered the institute spoke for about 20 minutes with the respective daughters and their mothers. In this, he was guided by a list of questions prepared in advance. The statements made by mothers and daughters (e.g., regarding weight) agreed much more with each other than we had originally expected.

The second follow-up inquiry of 1987 was almost exclusively conducted by one of us (G.W.). The disadvantage of his not being "blind" to the data seems to us to be outweighed by a great advantage: he had immersed himself deeply in the cases, had developed specific hypotheses about them, and, consequently, was able to ask specific questions. He was successful in inviting those 17 families who were living in the suburbs of Heidelberg to come to the institute and to make videotapes of the interviews he conducted with them. Five more families were willing to travel longer distances in order to have a live interview at our institute. With the remaining 20 families who were living at a greater distance from Heidelberg we conducted telephone conversations which were carefully recorded. Altogether we talked 6 times with the mother, 12 times with the identified patient and the mother, once with the identified patient and the father, and once with the identified patient, father, and mother. In all the families we questioned in 1984, we checked out the answers by comparing them with those made in 1987. We found that the statements made in the 1984 study agreed to a large extent with those made in the later study. Also, we found in each case major agreement between statements made independently by mothers and daughters.

In sum, we were able to establish contact with all 42 families we had included in the later study. In one case a mother refused more detailed information and referred us to the daughter who, now an adult, could tell us what we needed to know.

As expected, we were able to assess reasonably well the development of the young women under study with respect to somatic as well as psychosocial areas. These were:

1. eating behavior
2. weight
3. menstruation
4. individuation from family of origin
5. relationships with peers
6. development of relationships within the family
7. presence or absence of complaints and symptoms in other family members

Accordingly, we mainly asked questions referring to the above areas. Also, we were interested to learn whether further professional help had been used after the termination of the family sessions. In addition, we gathered information in several other areas which we considered relevant and about which we had formed hypotheses. These were, for example, the triggering situation, sibling rivalry, the family's attitudes about work and achievement and the nature and strength of the cohesion occurring between the children, parent, and grandparent generation. The live interviews lasted between one and two hours, the telephone conversations 15–30 minutes per person.

After the interviews the researcher assessed the patient and her family situation by means of seven scales, giving them ratings between #0 and #3. Here, 0 signified functionality and 3 marked dysfunctionality (for a detailed description of these scales see Appendix, pp. 227–230).

RELIABILITY OF RATINGS

In order to check the reliability of the above-mentioned seven scales, audiotapes and videotapes of 10 families were used. First ratings were carried out at various points in time by the original interviewer—first and last family interview and follow-up interview—and repeated six weeks later with the same families. A second independent rater rated the same families using the same tapes.

Inter- as well as intra-rater reliability was found to be high in all seven categories as measured by the Kendall-Tau Coefficient (p = 0.01), thus suggesting a high degree of stability of the rated variables over time.

RESULTS

We first present those results in the above areas that we ourselves consider most interesting. After that, we present four case histories in the light of our follow-up questioning. Finally, we try to summarize the results as well as our major impressions. We start with eating behaviors.

1. Eating Behaviors

When the joint family sessions began, 34 (80.95%) of our patients showed a marked disturbance of their eating behavior (rating #3). Such a disturbance was still observable in 20 (47.6%) of these patients at the end of the family sessions. While the family interviews went on, only minimal improvements between two bordering categories could be noted. On the whole we found that deviant eating habits tend to persist over a longer period of time even when there are significant changes and developments in other areas. At the end of the maximum follow-up period, only eight (19.05%) were assessed as belonging to rating #3. The time at which changes occurred seemed in no way to correlate with the follow-up period. Changes in eating behaviors appear possible at any time, even when deviances have persisted for many years (see Figure 6).

2. Weight

At the beginning of the family interviews 32 out of 42 patients (76.1%) weighed 25% less than their ideal weight. While the

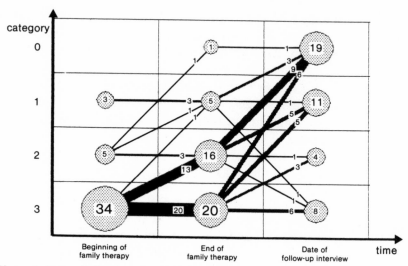

Figure 6. Eating behavior of identified patients.

family therapy went on, only 11 patients (26.19%) showed a change in weight that would have been sufficient to put them into the next-lower category. This, however, must be evaluated with caution. A girl of 18 years who, at the beginning of therapy, measures 1.74 meters (5′ 8½″) and weighs 38 kilograms (87 pounds) could gain more than 8 kilograms (18 pounds) and still stay in rating #3. The average weight gain during the family interviews amounted to 2.52 kilograms (5.5 pounds), while the girls grew on average by 0.17 centimeters (0.07″) during the same period. Twenty-one out of 42 girls (50%) did not gain any weight during the family sessions. Statistically there was no correlation between minimal weight and weight gain. Accordingly, a very low minimal weight (e.g., below 60 pounds) would give no indication of future weight gain. At the time of the follow-up interview only five young women (11.9%) were in rating #3, but only 16 (38.1%) in the rating #0 (from 15% above to 15% below normal weight). Accordingly, many of these young women continued to watch their weight and succeeded in keeping it approximately 15% below their ideal weight, notwithstanding their otherwise positive psychosocial development. On the average, all patients gained 10.59 kilograms (23.30 pounds) (and grew during the same period by 2.57 centimeters) (see Figure 7).

3. Menstruation

At the beginning of the family interviews, 35 of the 42 girls and young women (83.33%) were in rating #3 (secondary amenorrhea or primary amenorrhea that was not age-adequate). At the end of the family sessions, 31 (71.43%) were still in this rating. This agrees with our clinical experience, namely that reappearance of menstruation is usually delayed and follows in the wake of other changes.

At the end of the maximum follow-up period, only 9 (21.42%) were not menstruating, whereas 23 (59.52%) had a normal (or nearly normal) menstrual cycle. The longer the follow-up period, the more normalization is to be expected. In the group with the maximum follow-up period of 51–120 months, there had been an improvement of the menstrual cycle in 17 out of 22 cases (77.27%) (see Figure 8).

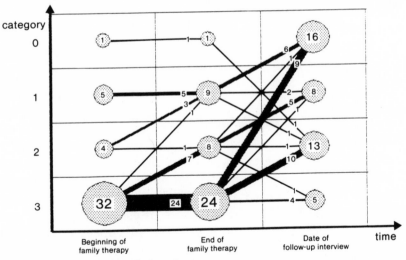

Figure 7. Weight of identified patients.

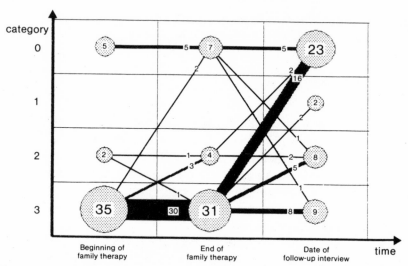

Figure 8. Menstruation of identified patients.

If we consider only those eight young women whose menstruation had been consistently absent during the whole period of observation, we find that they were on the average 20.3 years old when therapy started. Accordingly, by that time their anorectic symptoms had existed on average for four years and seven months. Hence, they were approximately two years older than the rest of the sample and had also been anorectic much longer. In seven out of these eight cases the anorexia seems to have been triggered by a traumatic loss or separation (five times the death or the serious illness of a close relative).

4. Individuation of the Identified Patients Vis-à-vis Their Families of Origin

The large majority of all patients in our sample at the beginning of family therapy (35 = 83.33%) were assessed as markedly under-individuated (rating #2 and #3). This assessment does not con-tradict the finding that a number of them appeared also to be parentified, that is, preoccupied with caring for their parents. While the family sessions lasted, 10 of them made clear progress in their individuation (change to the next rating). At the end of the follow-up period the proportion of young women who had individuated in accordance with their age had increased from five to 25 (59.5% reaching rating #0). At that time only eight (19.5%) remained in the #2 and #3 ratings (see Figure 9).

In our follow-up interviews with the formerly anorectic patients, we were told again and again that they considered the move out of the parental home to be a decisive step toward individuation. However, most of these young women also thought that the process of separation and individuation was a rather slow movement with many small steps forward and not a few backward. This was also felt to be the case by those patients who did not come for further professional help.

5. Relationships with Peers

We were surprised to find that it was in the area of relationships with peers that positive changes were most likely to occur while the family sessions were still going on. At the time of the first family interview, 39 out of 42 patients (92.86%) showed distinct

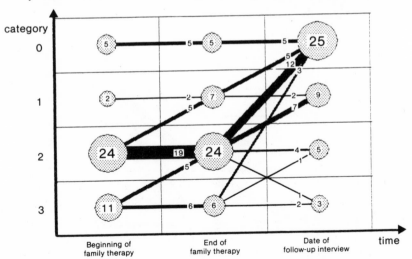

Figure 9. Individuation of identified patients vis-à-vis their families.

difficulties in their relationships with peers or had given up such relationships altogether. Sixteen girls (38.09%) improved their relationships with peers (and siblings) while the family therapy was still going on. Only 5 (11.90%) continued to show marked difficulties at the time of the follow-up interview (rating #3). Thirty-three (78.57%) had peer relationships appropriate for their age or were in the process of establishing them. During the family sessions we had already gained the impression that new movements in family relationships were frequently heralded by the girls' resuming contacts with old friends (of both sexes). However, the family members themselves frequently failed to pay attention to this, particularly in situations where symmetrical interactions prevailed (see Figure 10).

If we consider only those four young women whom we placed in rating #3 throughout the whole period of observation, we find the following characteristics:

- all four received subsequent treatment
- up to the time of the first family interview they had shown symptoms for a mean time span of 87 months (compared with 39 months in the rest of the sample)

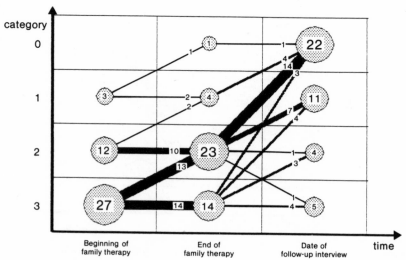

Figure 10. Relationship with peers.

- at the time of the first interview their average age was 23 years and 3 months (more than five years older than the sample as a whole)
- in three out of these four cases a sudden loss of contact with peers caused by illness or disappointment in a friendship were reported as triggering factors. In addition, each of the three saw a connection between their separation from their parents or the loss of a parent and the date their symptoms first appeared.

6. Development of Family Relationships

These assessments agree more or less with the way in which Beavers (1977) has determined the functionality/dysfunctionality of families. At the time of the first family interview, we assessed 39 (92.86%) of the families in our sample as dysfunctional or markedly dysfunctional (ratings #2 and #3). These assessments do not reflect any kind of enduring pathology. Rather, they describe a situation that has often arisen out of years of futile efforts, disappointments, and anxieties. In only nine of the 39 cases with the ratings #2 and #3 (23.038%) was there evidence of improvement while the family therapy was still going on. However, at the time of the last follow-up interview, 31 (73.8%) could be assessed as ranging from predominantly functional to mildly dysfunctional (ratings #0 and #1). Therefore, during the time of the follow-up, 28 out of 33 families with ratings #2 and #3 (84.85%) had improved with respect to the family's interactions (see Figure 11).

Development of the parental relationship. In Chapter 3 we introduced the concept of family-wide coindividuation and coevolution as a framework for assessing developments within the family life cycle. Our follow-up study was helpful in investigating the relevance and limits of this concept with respect to anorexia families. Our clinical impression that such family-wide coindividuation and coevolution can be quite uneven was confirmed.

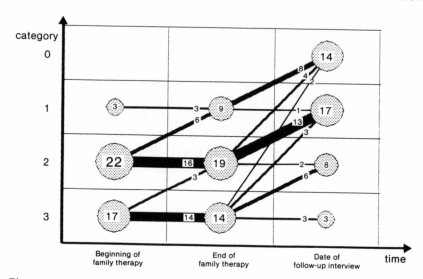

Figure 11. Functionality vs. dysfunctionality of families.

Indeed, we noted that certain family members tend to make more progress in their individuation than others. This applied in particular to the parents' relationship with each other. We usually found that here few, if any, noteworthy changes had occurred by the end of the therapy.

In order to assess the parental relationship at various points in time we made use of a rating scale with the following five dimensions:

1 = parents with a high measure of interaction, which the partners experience as positive and enriching, i.e., a parental relationship with a high degree of related individuation

2 = a good partner relationship with joint ventures carried out independently of the children

3 = a solid, reliable relationship with relatively little emotional exchange; rather, the partners seem to have a social partnership that is matter of fact and mainly centered on the joint care of children and/or grandparents

4 = a permanently stressful partnership; either a tense "parallel" living or frequent and repetitive arguments

5 = "trench warfare," or pending or actual breakup of the marriage through separation or divorce

On this scale we rated the marital relationship in 36 out of 39 families within ratings #3 to #5 at the beginning of the family therapy.

In three out of 42 families the father had died before the beginning of the family sessions. In each case, there was a close relationship between his death and the first appearance of anorectic symptoms in the daughter. In one case the parents were already divorced at the beginning of the family sessions, in two cases the parents separated during the course of the family therapy, and in one case they separated during the interval between the end of therapy and the time of the follow-up interview. (We found that in all these seven cases the girls had displayed vomiting as a symptom.)

All in all there were few changes in the above scale over the whole period of observation. Out of 17 marital relationships which were initially given rating #3, 15 were still there at the time of the final follow-up interview. If there were changes, they tended to occur between the end of family therapy and the end of the follow-up. Here the marital pairs changed from rating #4 to rating #3. This could be an indication of some movement in these couples. However, it is also possible that along with the decrease in the daughter's symptoms there were also fewer tensions in the parental relationship without any basic changes occurring. Out of the 17 cases who were assessed over a period from 24 to 50 months, only two (11.67%) showed a change for the better. Of the 22 cases which we were able to observe over 51–120 months, nine (40.91%) revealed positive changes. This may reflect the fact that these mostly centripetal and child-oriented families tend to need more time than other families to find a new, satisfying marital equilibrium after their children have left the home. (See Figure 12.)

A word of caution about the above observations: our scales may reflect criteria by which professional upper-middle-class peo-

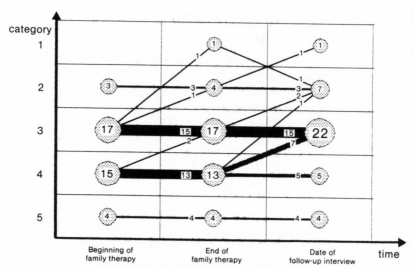

Figure 12. Parents' marital relationship.

ple (such as ourselves) evaluate the quality of a marital relationship. In other social classes and under different socioeconomic conditions other norms may well prevail and consequently other forms of marital relationships.

7. Symptoms and Complaints of Other Family Members

Many family therapists assume that another family member will develop symptoms as soon as the identified patient becomes symptom free. Therefore, they do not so much expect a removal of symptoms as an (intrafamilial) displacement of symptoms. We examined our data with a view to validating this assumption. However, we found no basis for confirmation. On the contrary, whereas at the beginning of the family interviews there were 11 families (26.19%) in which one or more members showed serious symptoms in addition to those of the identified patient, at the time of the follow-up this was true of only three families (7.14%). There was not one case in which another family member had developed new symptoms or had shown an aggravation of existing ones during the time of the family therapy. Five such cases arose between the end of the family therapy and the date of the final questioning. However, each time it was only a move from rating #0 to #1. In sum, at the end of the observation period there were 26 families (61.9%) in which the members were free of serious and/or persistent physical symptoms (see Figure 13).

A Note on Those Families with Whom Only One Interview Took Place

There were six families in our sample with whom we conducted only one interview. There were a variety of reasons for this. In three cases it had been known beforehand that there would be only one consultation. Two of these families lived a very long distance away and in the other family there was the added complication of the identified patient having already made plans for a new job in a different city. In another case, shortly after the first family interview the identified patient moved to her grandmother's in Northern Germany for an extended period. Two families said they had not returned because they didn't see much

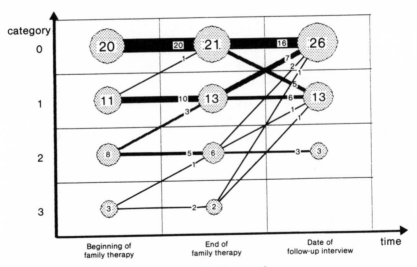

Figure 13. Symptoms found in other family members.

sense in further sessions and had been turned off by our setting with the one-way mirror and videotaping.

In two of these six families who were seen only once by us, the daughters did not seek any further treatment. We had told these two families almost the same thing at the end of the first interview, namely, that we were aware of difficulties but were also firmly convinced that they, as a family, had already taken the first steps toward finding a constructive solution and that no further professional help was needed. At the time of the follow-up interview these families clearly remembered what had been said at that time. They emphasized that this had been of great relevance to them.

Inpatient and Outpatient Treatments After the End of the Family Sessions

Out of the 42 patients in our sample, there were 12 (28.6%) who underwent inpatient treatment after the end of the family therapy (two-thirds of them on one occasion, one-third on two or more occasions). Before the beginning of the family sessions most of these (seven) had been treated in a general hospital. After the family therapy treatment had taken place, in most cases they entered psychiatric hospitals. There was no statistically measurable correlation ragarding in- and outpatient status before and after the family sessions. Out of 42 patients there were 19 (45.23%) who after the end of the family therapy took advantage of various forms of individual, group, and family consultation or therapy. These patients underwent on the average 1.5 treatments, 9 times individual therapy, 5 times individual consultation with fewer than 12 sessions, 6 times individual consultations with more than 12 sessions, 3 times participation in a self-help group, 3 times in family therapy, once in group therapy, and once psychiatric consultation. Twenty patients (47.6%) did not avail themselves of any further treatment after the end of the family sessions.

These findings are not easy to interpret. Normally the fact that there were subsequent treatments is taken to mean that the original treatment was not sufficiently effective. And absence of subsequent treatments is believed to reflect the efficacy of the original therapy. However, both views are open to question.

The fact that there were no further treatments can also mean that the family members withdrew into themselves and stayed entrenched in their dysfunctional patterns. And further individual therapy or consultation can mean a step toward individuation. Our follow-up interviews taught us how imperfectly the two above-mentioned views seem to fit the complex reality. For example, a patient whom we saw with her family for the first time in 1980 told us at the follow-up interview that the two therapists had very clearly emphasized the family's overly strong cohesion and its isolation from the environment by the way they put their questions. However, these questions implying the possibility of separation had been experienced as so threatening that the family closed ranks against the therapists and broke off any further contact. It was only years later that the patient realized what had taken place at that time. In another family we feel we succeeded in triggering decisive changes in the identified patient. Later on this patient studied psychology and participated in various self-help and encounter groups because of her professional interest. In our statistics, these activities figure as psychotherapies. However, at that time, she no longer needed help with those problems which once had brought her to our institute. Meanwhile, she had mostly given up her anorectic behavior, had separated from her parents, and had established good contacts with peers.

FOLLOW-UP INTERVIEWS

A. Sylvia Singer

In Chapter 8 we presented the first interview with the Singer family. Here we present a summary of the follow-up interview with the mother and the daughter Sylvia.

Sylvia was 19 years old when the family sessions began. Symptoms of anorexia nervosa, especially frequent vomiting, had first appeared when she was 15. Over a period of four months we conducted three family interviews. A major theme of the sessions was the function that Sylvia's anorectic behavior may have served with respect to the parents' troubled relationship and to blocking age-appropriate steps toward individuation. Also, we focused on the rivalry between the women vis-à-vis the father and on Sylvia's wish to be close to and accepted by her perfectionistic father. In addition, there was discussion about her simultaneous loyalty to her mother, whom she perceived as being dominated by her father. We interpreted her rather casual friendship with a boy in Amsterdam as evidence of her readiness to forgo a closer relationship that might have taken her away from her family. We suggest that the reader look once more at our final comments at the end of the first interview (see pp. 144–145).

We conducted our follow-up inquiry 25 months after our third (and last) session with the Singer family. We first telephoned the mother. We learned from her that Sylvia had married at the end of the previous year and was expecting a baby. The relationship with the boyfriend in Amsterdam had ended rather quickly. The mother said: "He was the clinging type. This made her afraid. He gave her no breathing space."

"After the family sessions we had some rather rough times. My husband was sent to Berlin by his firm and Sylvia didn't want to come along. Everything in the house was ready for her. But just when we were about to move she said: 'I'm just not going.' Instead, she moved in with her new boyfriend in his parents' house. Two weeks later her eating became normal. Everything was okay and the vomiting stopped, too."

Her boyfriend's mother took care of her. Initially, the mother said, Sylvia had continued to watch her figure. But then she became less obsessive and had gained 22 pounds by the time she became pregnant. Her menstruation had normalized before that. Mother said: "We remember your mentioning casually at one of the sessions that her weight and menstruation would no longer be a problem as soon as she found a suitable partner. Now we hope it will stay this way."

Regarding Sylvia's relationships with peers, her mother reported that sometime after the end of the family sessions Sylvia became very much involved with a group of kids doing karate. The parents didn't like that at all. Sylvia started to smoke and drink excessively with this group. However, she gave that up completely once she became pregnant. It was in this group that she met her future husband. Mother was then asked: "How did Sylvia relate to you as parents?" and she said: "For a while the relationship was not so good. That was shortly after she met her husband." However, even then Sylvia would call her mother from time to time, and at night, and ask her to come over. When this happened, the mother would always go. She would never think of ever leaving Sylvia on her own. Mother then said: "Now I'm holding myself back a little more. For a while Sylvia tried to have a closer relationship with my husband, her father. He went along with that. She also told him to visit her without telling me anything about it. But I know about this and just accepted it without mentioning it to her. Now our relationship is good; everything seems to be going normally." To the question: "How is your life in Berlin?" she responded: "I've gotten used to living there. Twice a month I still go over to Düsseldorf to help my parents for four or five days in their business. My oldest daughter is in Würzburg at the moment. Johann plans to return to West Germany after he's completed his high school exams. I still don't have a group of friends. But that takes time, I'm coping okay with the children leaving home. Over the Easter vacation my husband and I were by ourselves all the time. Before that we'd gone on a lot of vacations together. That went reasonably well. We're managing. (laughs) Well, after 25 years we should learn how to get along with each other. All in all, I'm glad that things have calmed down. Johann appreciates that, too. Right now he's staying with Sylvia. This is just one of several visits he's made recently. A little while ago he told me that he thought Sylvia was doing well and that she was happy. Basically, she now seems to be the way she was when she was 10—easygoing, laughing, and outgoing. The bad times of the anorexia now seem like an unhappy interlude. Things are taking their normal course again. She said herself that she wouldn't want to go through that again. And she has reassured us that she has no intention whatsoever of getting back into that situation."

We learned that Sylvia's husband was a few years older than she and that as an only child he was not without his problems. When visiting Sylvia, Sarah had felt that Sylvia was clinging to him and that he would like to have more freedom. Sylvia's mother-in-law was astonished: "I can't believe it. I've never seen my son be such a homebody!" Sylvia, again according to Sarah, was spending a lot of time by herself as her husband was running away from her. Then the mother said: "Sarah feels that there are problems in store for them. Yet I am confident that once she has her child she will have something to hold on to. Before she got pregnant she got herself a rabbit so as to have something for herself. She was also working up until the last minute. Before she got to know her husband I was afraid things would go downhill. I was always on the verge of calling her. But then I told myself: Let's wait a little longer. But I must confess there were times when I was holding my breath."

Sylvia Singer reported: "Things went fine from the moment I told myself I can manage by myself. Now I'm married and I'm having a baby *(laughs)*. It couldn't be better. No more problems with not wanting to eat. On the contrary. I knew the solution would be not moving in with my parents. And that's how it happened."

To the question: "Since when have you allowed yourself to feel well?" Sylvia responded: "Things have been going well for 18 months. It happened when I got to know my husband and moved into an apartment in his parents' house. After that I gained 24 pounds within three months. Later I added another five pounds. I simply forgot to think about eating. And I stopped vomiting from one day to the next." To the question: "How did you do that?" she responded: "I honestly don't know. Suddenly, it didn't have any importance any longer. Perhaps I needed it as a kind of substitute gratification or to distract myself from something. Anyway, it was fantastic. I was surprised myself. I knew that I could do it but it had never crossed my mind that it would go so well, so smoothly. Thank heaven it happened this way. I don't like to think what might have happened otherwise."

Apart from the trivial things that can upset any relationship temporarily, she saw herself as getting along well with her husband. She said: "I did the right thing when I refused to move to Berlin with my parents, when I took a stand." She noted delayed development in her siblings. She felt that her brother, in particular, was holding back too much, saying: "He can't be free, can't be himself, because he's still under the thumb of our parents. He thinks he has to be something special and always in top form because his father is a managing director."

To the question: "How did your parents react to your separation?" she responded: "The parents were surprised and at first resisted it. But I told them in no uncertain terms what I wanted. I gave up my apartment and moved in with my boyfriend. I told them that over the telephone. At first they were totally nonplussed. And there wasn't much they could do about it. This was totally new behavior for them. They had always seen me as a fragile, beloved, darling little girl. But when I was a teenager it had already become evident that I might turn out to be the stronger of us girls and that I would do what I want. Of course, that was also the root of my problems and got me into the anorexia nervosa. As I told you, my father stands there dumbstruck and simply cannot grasp that such things can happen. But, of course, he's also happy that things are turning out well. Initially he didn't even register that he is about to become a grandfather."

To the question: "How are the parents now getting along with each other?" she responded: "I don't know much about that really. It's no longer much of a concern to me. Basically, there's still a lot of tension. I don't think that things have improved that much. When I talk with my mother on the phone she hints that there are disagreements with my father. But then I let her know that I don't want to talk about it. After all, it's become clear that both of them are not interested in bringing about major changes. And so they shouldn't bother me with their problems. At the beginning it wasn't easy to tell them that in such clear terms. But it had to be. Do you think I should continue to burden myself with my parents' problems? No, never!"

Sylvia then mentioned that she had canceled further family sessions after the third one because her brother and father had no longer seemed motivated to travel such long distances. Finally she also reached the decision to do without further professional help. She said: "That's the only way to do it." At the end of the conversation she brought up what one therapist had told her at the end of a session. She said: "He expressed doubts that I could do it. Please give him my regards and tell him what I've achieved."

B. Christa Bremer

Christa Bremer was 28 years old when she arrived with her parents for the first family interview. The three lived in northern Germany and had to travel about 250 miles. Christa had recently undergone her seventh course of inpatient treatment because of her anorexia nervosa, as well as alcohol and drug dependence. She had had acute kidney failure and she had to be given an artificial kidney.

Christa began to have difficulties when she was 15 years old. At that time the maternal grandmother, who was living with the family, fell seriously ill. She had been the center of the family and had been nicknamed the "warm family stove." After the grandmother's death Christa's parents had more arguments with each other. Her two sisters left the parental home, married, and started families of their own. Christa, however, returned home after a first attempt at separation failed.

Between 1981 and 1983 we conducted a total of eight family interviews with this family. We questioned Christa and her mother by telephone in the context of our follow-up study first 24 and later 63 months after the end of the family sessions. In the following we present some of the statements Christa and her mother made during the second follow-up interview. Then we briefly discuss the family's progress since the end of the family sessions.

Christa reported over the telephone that she had been married for two years and that she was doing "terrifically." Thereupon the therapist said: "How did you manage that?" Christa replied: "I don't know, really. I think my husband has helped me a lot. He has given me plenty of love. He knew practically everything about me and never let himself be put off by that knowledge. He always let me know that he loved me just the way I was:

dumping food into myself, drinking like hell, and throwing up. He says now that once in a while for him, too, there were times when he was ready to give up. But that never came across to me. I always felt that he believed in me and he believed that I would get over it all. Overall he had a totally different picture of me than I had of myself. And eventually I took it over from him.

"But it also had to do with the therapy we had with you. I remember that therapy as something very positive. It was very different from other therapies I'd experienced.

"After the therapy my parents held themselves back a lot. They let me do my own thing and no longer bothered me. That relieved me a great deal and I no longer had any reason to be greatly concerned with them. Really, they went their separate ways and got along well with each other. That was the most important thing. Of course, it was also painful that I had to let go of my parents. But I did have my husband. It was also important for me that I was living in Bonn by myself. That meant I was separated from my parents. Now I'm alive again; before, I was dead."

Upon questioning, Christa reported that she had turned vegetarian and that her eating habits were normal. For two years she had not been vomiting at all. Her menstrual cycle was normal and regular and she had also given up drinking. She said: "That's been over for more than two years. I no longer smoke, I no longer drink, I no longer go on binges, and I no longer throw up. My husband has also stopped drinking. He did this some time before I myself stopped bingeing."

During the family sessions Christa had reported having major difficulties in her relationships with others, so we broached this subject, too. She said: "I've also improved in this respect. I continue to be a little shy and to be anxious about close relationships. I'm making progress in little stages. But I've found out that I enjoy having relationships with others and I've become aware that there are things I can give to others. But it can't go too fast. Otherwise I'll flip out and react with my body." When asked: "Even with your husband?" she replied: "Yes, with him, too. I think he also has problems in regulating closeness and distance. You see it's not always sweetness and light between us. We have our fights and then we make up again. Because of my husband's job, at present we only see each other on weekends. But that's not a bad solution for either of us. I'm not sure we would manage if we were together day in and day out." She reported further that both of them enjoyed sex. In the long run they also planned living together full time. But her first priority was to complete her studies. Both also had plans to eventually have children. To the question: "How do you now relate to your body?" she responded: "Very differently from the way I used to. I feel well in a very new way and think it's wonderful to feel warm and relaxed."

She also mentioned that she was getting along well with her parents and her siblings. After all, the sibling relationship was never unduly problematic. To the question: "How do the parents manage without the daughter?" she responded: "Better than with her. They have a good life together. It's really astonishing what the two of them have achieved together. They now have excellent relationships with all their children and grandchildren. Occasionally they still have arguments. I saw that when I was at home. Before, I couldn't stand that at all. It used to drive me crazy. So it was such a lucky thing that we ended up with you."

In the telephone conversation with Christa's mother, the mother confirmed that the family was doing well. She said: "Recently Christa spent six months with us when she was doing a traineeship in our town. She slept in our house but otherwise looked after herself. I didn't cook for her. That was her job. But we had meals together." To the question: "How did you get along with each other?" she responded: "It was great, not at all like in the old times. We got along well with each other. It's such a difference. At present, she's going back to her studies in Bonn. In June, during the summer vacation, she plans to serve as a trainee in England. Well, the girl has big plans. As regards her appearance and her body, she now looks very well." She confirmed Christa's statements regarding weight, menstruation, and eating behavior. To the question: "How about alcohol?" she responded: "That's finished. She's stopped drinking altogether. She no longer needs it. We hardly recognize her as the same person. She's also married, as you may know."

We also learned from the mother that her husband had recently had some problems with his stomach without any organic cause having been found. When asked: "How are you getting along with your husband?" she said: "Occasionally we have fights. At the moment we're getting along fine."

When asked about the family sessions, she responded: "We're glad that someone like you exists. That was a very positive therapy, the only right way. After all, we were totally at a loss as to how we could get out of this mess. Certainly, we wanted to do something and wanted to do it right. But we were kind of stuck. That was such an unhappy situation."

Some reflections by the therapists. When the parents and Christa came to their first family interview they were enmeshed in repetitive and restrictive interactional circles. Understandably the parents had been shocked when Christa, an inpatient again, could only survive by means of an artificial kidney. Thus they continued to watch her anxiously and closely after her discharge from the hospital. Christa, for her part, felt responsible for the well-being and the cohesion of the parents. This led to her losing all contacts with the outside world. Her only relationship outside her family was the one with her fiancé. But that was problematic because of the latter's alcoholism.

In the triad that was formed by the parents and Christa there existed strong differences and tensions. The father had had a much closer relationship with Christa. The mother reacted to this with jealousy and a feeling of being excluded and disapproved of. She had had similar feelings in her own family of origin when her parents had favored her brother. Also, Mr. and Mrs. Bremer could not imagine how they should deal jointly with Christa's behavior. For example, the father supported Christa's desire to cook for the family since he thought that this was better than not doing anything at all. The mother, however, felt pushed out of what she considered to be her domain.

What use were the family interviews? When we asked ourselves this question in the light of the original family sessions and the follow-up interviews, we reached the following—tentative—conclusions:

1. We succeeded, probably through positive connotations and reframings, in reducing guilt feelings, activating a new sense of self-worth and competence, and providing the family with a new sense of direction.
2. Very likely we were helpful in separating the generations from each other, for example, by setting up a few sessions in which we saw the parents and Christa and Christa and a sister separately, and by requesting the parents to spend one week on vacation without calling home about Christa's well-being.
3. We believe we helped the parents to find a rapprochement as marital partners. This, in turn, made it easier for Christa to develop initiatives of her own.
4. Very probably we helped the family, through our hypothetical and mainly future-oriented questions, to find new perspectives on how to conduct their lives in a meaningful and hopeful manner.

However, there was no doubt in our minds that conditions for a successful therapy were extremely favorable. All family members had been shocked by Christa's acute kidney failure and the threat of death. They knew that things couldn't go on as they were. At the time of the first follow-up interview Christa said: "The decisive event and trigger for all that followed was the kidney failure. Before that I had allowed myself to drift." Also the vacation that we ordered the parents to take seems to have contributed to positive progress. The parents experienced this vacation as their second honeymoon. However, before they started it, we had alerted them, via a number of questions, to the numerous ways in which they could prevent themselves from having a good time.

Christa was one of the patients to take advantage of further therapy after the end of the family sessions. Because of her fear that she might take to drinking again, she participated for two years in a self-help group. Also, a few years after the end of family therapy, she had some sessions of individual therapy provided by a counseling service. She experienced these sessions as useful, supportive, and stabilizing. Even though the interviewing therapist had been confident the family could and would use their own resources, he was surprised and moved by the extent to which they had done so in the intervening years.*

C. Paula Andres

In 1983, at the age of 27 years, Paula Andres came to the first family interview, together with her 54-year-old mother. She was in a pitiful condition: 5' 3" tall, she weighed a mere 55 pounds. Mother and daughter were both without jobs. They lived in separate apartments but saw each other daily. Except for physicians they hardly had any contacts with the outside world. Paula's family physician wrote us: "Repeated inpatient treatments have been failures. From the point of view of organic medicine I can recommend outpatient treatment despite a body weight of 55 pounds."

When the two women discussed their lives, they talked mainly about losses. Except for a distant relative with whom they had only infrequent contact, they saw themselves as the sole survivors of their family. They said: "None of us can now survive alone. . . . In death we will be reunited."

When Paula was born in 1956, her maternal grandmother died. At that time, Paula's birth was not welcome. When she was three years old her father died of stomach cancer, and a short time thereafter his two only brothers died, also of cancer. Mother and

---

* Just before this book went to press, Christa and her husband presented themselves for a live follow-up interview at our institute, made possible by a business trip for the husband. The interview took place 75 months after the end of the family sessions. Essentially, the spouses confirmed the picture we had gained of them through the telephone interview: Both had continued to abstain from drinking alcohol and both saw themselves as getting along well with each other, despite occasional quarrels. There was one—to us—interesting additional piece of information: Christa said she had given up vomiting the very moment she had made herself financially independent from her father.

daughter moved in with the paternal grandparents, who were seen as having suffered losses and, therefore, needing support. Paula loved and adored her grandmother. For her she was a saint. Soon after this grandmother's death Paula began to show symptoms of anorexia nervosa. This resulted in both the mother and daughter becoming even more tied to each other. They managed to separate only when Paula lost too much weight. That happened when she weighed less than 44 pounds and her life was in jeopardy. She was then admitted to a hospital and fed until she could go home again. She saw hospitalization not as a help but as a constraint from which she tried to free herself. As soon as she returned home she started losing weight again. The cycle of hospitalizations and discharges with the corresponding ups and downs in her weight turned into a ritual. When she was out of the hospital, she presented a grotesque sight. Yet she continued to drive a car and to make herself visible by sitting in a cafe. Inevitably she became the center of much attention. Yet she seemed to enjoy this and emphasized that she didn't want to be a grey mouse like all the rest of mankind. Soon the mother and daughter could no longer imagine being separated from each other for more than half a day. Each would have felt it a breach of trust if she could not carry with her the keys to the other's apartment at all times. The constant threat of death (or play with death) tied the two of them more and more closely together. Neither seemed able or willing to survive by herself.

Over a period of eight months the two experienced therapists conducted a series of sessions with both women, and a few with the mother alone. At first they were quite successful in building up a supportive relationship. But neither positive connotations nor the confirmation of the status quo nor tasks aimed at strengthening the boundaries between them proved effective in bringing about lasting changes. After a first hopeful phase in which the mother courageously embarked on her own individuation, she abruptly canceled any further sessions. This happened at a time when Paula had been sent to a hospital, once more weighing 41 pounds.

Forty-five months after the end of the family sessions, we invited Paula and her mother to come to Heidelberg for a follow-up interview. Paula said then that she would have liked to visit us but did not feel well enough to make the trip. Seven months later we had another extensive telephone interview with her and her mother. By that time she was totally bedridden.

We learned that since the last family session she had been hospitalized twice. Paula said: "They filled me up with tubes and infusions and so got my weight up. But once I was discharged I managed to get my weight down again."

At the time of the last telephone interview, mother and daughter saw themselves at a dead end. They also felt that the doctors had given up on them. There were still occasional visits by a family doctor but little was done by him.

About nine months after the end of the family sessions mother and daughter had rented a new apartment together. Following this, their quarrels had intensified and their isolation had increased. The mother said: "In this high-rise apartment building everything is very anonymous. There are four apartments on our floor. I don't remember when I last saw a neighbor." Paula said: "The apartment is too small. I feel cooped up like in a box. There is nobody around except for my mother. When we are together, we torture each other mercilessly. But when we are apart, it breaks my heart."

Both were longing for their former separate apartments. However, for financial reasons they could afford only one apartment. Recently Paula had been offered an inexpensive two-room apartment, but by then she could no longer live by herself. Paula said she presently weighed almost 41 pounds. She reported that her face and her legs were swollen with edema. She said: "I can't stop starving myself. Wherever I am, I have the scales in my head. It is terrible that I am holding on to life so tenaciously. There was a time when I weighed only 37 pounds (while measuring 5′ 3″) and yet I didn't die. My life consists of taking something in, getting something out, and my weight going up, my weight going down! I can't stop fasting but neither can I carry on as I do at the moment. We are constantly fighting over meals. I tremble when I hear mother returning from shopping. I'm always torn. On the one hand, I try to secretly throw out the food that my mother has prepared for me, to give it to the dog or to make it inedible by mixing it up with perfume and cosmetic creams. On the other hand, I feel again and again compelled to binge, devouring food without a knife or fork and oblivious to any manners. I can't vomit anymore, so I'm using laxatives." She categorically refused another hospitalization.

Of the family sessions the mother had this to say: "The therapists tried very hard. The advice they gave us was good but we didn't listen." And Paula added: "The sessions were no great help to me, but they benefited my mother. For her they were an eye-opener. For me, they were more like a talk show. The therapists were fun. But I caught on to their game. The one expressed himself this way, the other that way, but in the end it didn't make much difference. Neither could give really helpful advice."

Toward the end of the interview Paula reflected on her approaching death. She said: "My apartment is in the beyond. There is a garden where I can be happy. But my car is here and I don't know how to get from here to there."

In retrospect the therapists wondered whether they had pushed too hard for changes even though they (also) pleaded for the status quo. Perhaps it would have been better to respect the patient's decisions in a more clear-cut way, even though they, as therapists, could not view the patient's own solutions as optimal. Paula and her mother made us painfully aware of our limitations as therapists.

D. Ilse Jakob

Of the 62 young women on whom we have follow-up data, 11 (=17.7%) were only children. Ilse Jakob was one of them. We assessed 10 of these 11 families with only children as showing a strongly centripetal orientation. Almost all of them had only sparse contacts with the outside world. In nine of these families the anorectic girls had formed a very close coalition with their mothers against the fathers. The fathers were viewed as being authoritarian, dominating, peripheral, and/or involved in matters outside the family. In contrast to what we observed in many other families we studied, these coalitions were typically quite overt. Again and again we gained the impression that the mothers had suffered a painful loss (e.g., a parent) and that the daughter who later became anorectic had filled the empty place as a confidante, sister, and friend. Ilse Jakob's family also presented this constellation.

Ilse was 16 years old when she entered family therapy with her parents after treatment as an inpatient. The father was then 68 years old. He had lost his first wife in 1956 and had been living on social security for some time. He had only infrequent contact with his relatives. Ilse's mother, 52 years old at the time of the first family interview, was also an only child. She came from Hamburg, where her father, a successful publisher, died in 1945 at the end of World War II. The mother's mother suffered very much from the loss of her husband; at the same time she resented having to live more modestly. After a disappointing relationship with a professional man, the mother moved in with her mother in Hamburg. There she got to know Ilse's father. A few years after the wedding the mother's mother joined the family. Subsequently, the home became more lively and entertaining. The three women formed a kind of subculture within the family, while Ilse's father seemed married to his work and the television screen. When the grandmother died (the father retired almost simultaneously), Ilse and her mother closed ranks even more. Ilse tried from then on to replace the grandmother in the family. She prepared breakfast in the morning and stopped her mother from criticizing her father too harshly. (However, in the family sessions it was Ilse who frequently treated the father like a child. She said, for example: "Now keep quiet for a while! That's not your business! That's what bothers me about you!") Her symptoms began to show when she traveled to England and was first separated from the family for a longer period of time. Her mother, though, thought she herself suffered even more from the separation than Ilse. Ilse's anorectic behavior helped to reduce the tensions between her mother and father. At the same time the tie between the mother and daughter became even closer. They had many common interests such as music, theater, and the arts and had many deep conversations about them. This could also be seen as delegation: Ilse allowed the mother to experience vicariously what the mother would have liked to experience herself after the War.

The family broke off further interviews after the second session, in which the two therapists had repeatedly brought up the possibility of more separateness between the women. Ilse's reactions at that time were: "We are one family. We belong together. Leaving the family would be escapism."

At the time of the second follow-up interview (56 months after the end of the family sessions) Ilse's eating behavior seemed to have lost its relevance for the family relationships. She was an assiduous student of art history and languages and wanted to become an editor. She had hardly any peer relationships and was again living at home. Here the relationships seemed unchanged. Mother and daughter continued their intense relationship, while the father was marginal and often away on hikes. Mother said: "That's the way men are." She emphasized that nature had made men and women differently and therefore had destined them to have different types of relationships. In her family there existed a strong tradition of close relationships between women. Her own maternal grandmother had already emphasized the importance of mothers and daughters living in close proximity. Men were seen as a more-or-less necessary evil. The contacts the family had had with psychosocial institutions were seen in a rather negative light. In their view the family sessions had taken place at the wrong time. Physically, Ilse had been in very poor shape. There had been one more inpatient treatment after the family sessions but that had not done a thing for her, they said. However, the family saw a positive value in Ilse's later moving to a famous boarding school for girls. This school happened to be not far away from the family's home and the progress triggered by this change was seen as appropriate and timely.

Following this, Ilse's eating behavior improved. She resumed her contacts with peers and appeared more balanced and self-assured. However, we thought the mother was right when she remarked in the follow-up interview that Ilse still had some way to go. She would have to prove that she could earn a living, move into her own apartment, and live by herself. We think such a positive outcome will largely depend on whether mother and Ilse succeed in opening up their close relationship and supplement it with other relationships that are stable and enriching.

SUMMARY AND FINAL REFLECTIONS

The above case descriptions highlight our frequent difficulties when assessing therapeutic success or failure with anorectic girls and young women. Each time, the relational constellation differs from the start. Each time, too, we are intervening in the life cycle when complexly interwoven biological and psychosocial forces are already working toward change. And there remain, too, the above-mentioned methodological problems. And they will increase to the degree that we try to do justice both to the various intersecting causal chains and to the passage of time.

With these difficulties in mind, we tried nonetheless to arrive at some sort of a global estimate of the changes observed over the period under study. To this end we made use of the categories that had served as ratings on the seven scales described earlier. These four ratings were given a numerical value which indicated their range from 0 = largely functional to 3 = largely dysfunctional. Then we added up the numerical values in all seven areas. Thus we were able to allot one global value to each of the 42 families.

We are aware of the methodological problems in this procedure. They derive mainly from the unproven assumption that the intervals between the ratings 0–3 can be scaled evenly and that the assessments in all seven areas can be given equal global weight. But these objections notwithstanding, we feel such global assessment to be a justifiable and meaningful addition to the descriptions detailed earlier, the more so as it encompasses somatic features as well as individual and family dynamics. Table 3 shows the results.

If in using the four ratings we add up all the ratings of a given family, we get a sum that may range from 0 = very functional to 21 = very dysfunctional. If we then look at all the families, we find that at the time of the first interview, 39 (92.86%) of

Table 3

Ratings	At time of first family interview		At time of following interviews		Changes observable between time of first family interview and last follow-up interview		
	N	%	N	%	Improvement	Deterioration	No change
0 – 5	0	0	22	52.38		1	0
6 – 10	3	7.14	11	26.19	2	0	1
11 – 15	14	33.33	5	11.91	13	0	4
16 – 21	25	59.52	4	9.52	21		
	42	100.00	42	100.00	36	1	5

them had a rather dysfunctional rating, and of these a further 25 (59.52%) had a very dysfunctional rating. Not one family is to be found in the functional realm. This contrasts with the situation at the time of the follow-up interview. Now 33 (85.57%) families have the largely functional rating and of these, 22 (52.38%) have a very functional rating. Only two families (9.52%) continued to belong to the very dysfunctional group.

The movements between the various ratings during the period of observation thus indicate that 36 families (85.71%) changed in the direction of greater functionality. Five families (11.9%) did not show any movement at all. And in only one family (2.38%) was there a deterioration, that is, evidence of greater dysfunctionality.

What lessons are we then to draw from our follow-up study? In our opinion the most important are these:

1. In a phase of life such as adolescence and young adulthood, in which many changes are taking place as it is, we may quite often observe developments (e.g., in physical appearance, bodily processes, psychological attitudes and relationships) that strike us as astounding. Depending on the observer and his or her criteria, these may be seen as either positive or negative.

2. In order to facilitate positive developments, relatively short but intense interventions in a problem system may be highly effective. This is especially the case when the interventions happen to take place at a propitious moment in time.

3. We found confirmation of a general tendency frequently noted in the literature: namely, the longer restrictive patterns have been operating in the biological as well as psychosocial areas, the harder these are to change. Yet our study also taught us that even rigidly and enduringly entrenched patterns may have a lasting change in the wake of systemic interventions.

Our study also confirmed the well-known fact that various types of therapy may be useful with anorectic girls and young women. Therefore, we do not view family therapy as a panacea for all ills. However, we believe that in many situations there are good reasons to favor systemic therapy—which should not necessarily be equated with family therapy—over other therapies.

This applies in particular to situations in which we deal with strongly bound-up systems. These are, of course, in the first place those family systems in which the anorectic girls are still living at home and are subject to the binding forces described earlier. Our study suggests that in such systems it is not only the girl but all members who can benefit from family therapy. In the course of the therapies conducted by us, no other family members became ill; on the contrary, the health of these members improved in quite a number of cases.

This may have to do with the fact that the therapy we practice always has a dual thrust. It is, on the one hand, aimed at activating an individual's own motivation, including his or her ability and willingness to develop his or her own initiative and to accept responsibility for what he or she is doing. It does, on the other hand, take into consideration those systems forces that may thwart such individual motivation. We believe that in favorable cases this dual-track approach may potentiate therapeutic effectiveness. The systems that we consider relevant are not only families, but may also include professional helpers, institutions such as schools, and peer groups. And they may also be systems of ideas (or ideologies) (e.g., those that unduly glorify beauty, physical fitness, and achievement). Where such features of ideologies are internalized as basic assumptions never to be questioned, they become part of what we have called a "hard" relational reality. We think that such hard reality can be found in the majority of anorexia families. The constructivist approach elaborated in this book seems particularly suited to softening up such hard reality, thereby opening up new perspectives and chances for autonomous, future-oriented actions.

Many of the existing follow-up studies on eating disturbances can be seen as confirming a common assumption: about one-third of all anorectics recover spontaneously and the rest remain stuck with minor or major impediments. Recent works, such as those by Yager and colleagues (1987) and Hsu (1987), also confirm this assumption. However, in the light of our clinical experience, as well as of the follow-up study presented here, we see no reason for fatalism or resignation. Rather, we are confident that good outcomes can be facilitated in the great majority of cases. That, for us, is the most important message in this book.

Appendix

DESCRIPTION OF RATING SCALES

1. *Eating Behavior of Identified Patients*

0 = largely normal eating behavior
1 = some peculiarities in eating behavior such as unusual food choices; feeling uncomfortable when eating in the presence of others; a propensity to pressure others to eat more; excessive preoccupation with caloric intake; occasional vomiting (on the average once a month maximum); by and large, however, eating behavior has lost interactional significance.
2 = markedly dysfunctional eating behavior, relatively frequent and longer lasting periods of fasting with noticeable loss of weight; a propensity to binge; vomiting in tense situations (on the average no more than one or two times per week); a strong preoccupation with food and eating; marked weight phobias; repeated fights with family members over food and eating behavior.
3 = markedly disturbed eating behavior; persistent and marked reduction of food intake; massive bingeing followed by vomiting (on the average more than twice per week); constant preoccupation with food; marked weight phobias; frequent symmetrical interactions with family members over eating behavior.

2. Weight of Identified Patients

0 = between 15% below normal weight and 15% above normal weight
1 = up to 15% below ideal weight
2 = 15–25% below ideal weight
3 = more than 25% below ideal weight

3. Menstruation of Identified Patients

0 = mostly regular menstruation or age-appropriate primary amen-orrhea (up to 15 years of age)
1 = irregular (with intervals up to three months) and/or greatly varying menstrual bleeding
2 = longer periods of amenorrhea (intervals of more than three months); occasional occurrence of either very weak or very strong bleeding; menstruation triggered by medication in cases where it is doubtful whether it would have occurred without medication; menstruation occurring spontaneously up to the time when oral contraceptives were taken but stopping after discontinuation of contraceptives and only retriggered through hormones.
3 = primary amenorrhea which is not age-appropriate (after 15) secondary amenorrhea

4. Individuation of Identified Patients Vis-à-vis Their Families

0 = largely age-appropriate individuation
1 = moderately retarded development or some parentification as, for example, shown by a relationship with one or both parents that seems too intimate and confidential for the daughter's age; after a move away from home, daily and lengthy telephone conversations with the parents over longer periods of time; a strong orientation toward her family of origin that appears age-inappropriate; or a lasting parentification that also seems age-inappropriate.
2 = Marked delay of development or strong parentification as, for example, shown by the young girl's constant need for close contact with a parent; soliciting of the parents' recognition and

attention; acting much younger than would be appropriate for her age; or showing marked pseudo-autonomous behaviors—for example, moves out of the house repeatedly and hastily and, because of insufficient planning, soon finds herself back at home in a state of disillusionment and frustration.

3 = very marked underindividuation or compulsive pseudo-individuation—for example, showing markedly regressive and/or symbiotic behaviors; hanging on to mother's apron strings, unable to stay by herself; showing very infantile behaviors; or showing very marked overindividuation—for example, abruptly and persistently breaking off relationships with family members and appearing self-sufficient and unapproachable.

5. Relationships with Peers

0 = by and large, good and age-appropriate relationships with peers.
1 = has at least one emotionally sustaining relationship with a peer (girlfriend or boyfriend) or is in the process of actively building up such a relationship.
2 = marked difficulties in establishing and maintaining contacts, relationships with peers sporadic and fragile.
3 = marked retreat from peers, abruptly and persistently breaking off contacts, encapsulation, and isolation.

6. Relationships Within the Family of Origin

0 = relationships largely functional and in line with the family's socioeconomic status. Members see their relationships basically in positive terms, and are able and willing to resolve conflicts constructively, and so forth. Adequate and flexible boundaries, good emotional and intellectual exchange.
1 = on the whole, relationships appear moderately stressed and are seen frequently as problematical—for example, marked centripetal or centrifugal movements, prominence of a dyad within the family, markedly peripheral position of one member, repeated flare-ups of tension or longer periods of emotional distance.
2 = family relationships more obviously dysfunctional. For months at a time family members experience major difficulties—for example, persistent tensions; splittings; massive blurring of inter-

individual and generational boundaries; minimal emotional and intellectual exchange; formation of lasting coalitions.

3 = markedly dysfunctional family relationships which are experienced as extremely stressful—for example, feelings of extreme suffocation or alienation; strong and frequent symmetrical escalations; "trench warfare" or extreme avoidance of conflicts; marked communication deviances or very "hard" constructions of reality; extreme centripetal or centrifugal movements; persistent dilemmas.

7. Complaints, Symptoms, or Illnesses in Other Family Members at the Time of Interview

(We attached less importance to degenerative and/or chronic illnesses that existed before the appearance of the daughter's anorectic behavior and presumably were not affected by it and vice versa. Rather, we paid attention to symptoms that conceivably could have replaced the symptoms of anorexia and/or could have had major interactional significance in connection with that condition. We assessed only members of the nuclear family and those close relatives who maintained intensive and regular contacts with this family.)

0 = all family members experience themselves as predominantly healthy.

1 = apart from the identified patient, one other family member presents moderately severe symptoms such as bed wetting, stuttering, migraine headaches, stomach ulcers, phobias; or several family members present minor complaints such as allergic rhinitis, hives, back pains, vulnerability to infectious diseases, and so forth.

2 = apart from the identified patient, one other family member shows serious symptoms, such as severe obsessive-compulsive or psychotic behavior, cancer, suicide, multiple sclerosis, colitis, severe bronchial asthma; or several family members show symptoms of medium severity.

3 = several other family members present serious symptoms such as stroke *and* bone tuberculosis, psychoses *and* asthma, and so forth.

Bibliography

Al-Alami, M.S., Beumont, P.J.V., & Touyz, S.W. (1987). The further development of the concept of anorexia nervosa. In P.J.V. Beumont, G.D. Burrows, & R.C. Casper (Eds.), *Handbook of eating disorders. Part 1: Anorexia and bulimia nervosa*. Amsterdam, New York, Oxford: Elsevier.

American Psychiatric Association (1980). *Diagnostic and statistical manual of mental disorders, DSM-III* (3rd edition). Washington, DC: American Psychiatric Association.

American Psychiatric Association (1987). *Diagnostic and statistical manual of mental disorders, DSM-III-R* (3rd edition, revised). Washington, DC: American Psychiatric Association.

Andersen, H., Goolishian, H., & Winderman L. (1986). Problem determined systems: Towards transformation in family therapy. *Journal of Strategic and Systemic Therapies, 5*, 1–13.

Aponte, H., & Hoffman, L. (1973). The open door: A structural approach to a family with an anorectic child. *Family Process, 12*, 1–45.

Auerswald, E.H. (1971). Families, change, and the ecological perspective. *Family Process, 10*, 263–280.

Bateson, G. (1972). *Steps to an ecology of mind*. San Francisco: Chandler.

Bateson, G. (1979). *Mind and nature*. Toronto, New York, London: Bantam Books.

Bateson, G., Jackson, D.D., Haley, J., & Weakland, J.H. (1956). Toward a theory of schizophrenia. *Behavioral Science, I*, 251–264.

Beavers, W.R. (1977). *Psychotherapy and growth: A family systems perspective*. New York: Brunner/Mazel.

Beavers, W.R. (1981). A systems model of family for family therapists. *Journal of Marital and Family Therapy, 7,* 299–307.

Beavers, W. (1982). Healthy, midrange and severely dysfunctional families. In F. Walsh (Ed.), *Normal family processes.* New York: Guilford Press.

Beavers, W.R. (1985). *Successful marriage: A family systems approach to couples therapy.* New York: W.W. Norton.

Beavers, W.R., & Voeller, M. (1983). Comparing and contrasting the Olson Circumplex Model with the Beavers Systems Model. *Family Process, 22,* 85–98.

Blos, P. (1962). *On adolescence/A psychoanalytic interpretation.* New York: The Free Press.

Boscolo, L., Cecchin, G., Hoffman, L., & Penn, P. (1987). *Milan systemic family therapy: Conversations in theory and practice.* New York: Basic Books.

Boskind-Lodahl, M. (1976). Cinderella's stepsisters: A feminist perspective on anorexia nervosa and bulimia. *Signs, 2* (1), 120–146. Reprinted in J.H. Williams (Ed.), *Psychology of women: Selected readings* (pp. 436–448). New York: W.W. Norton, 1979.

Boszormenyi-Nagy, I., & Krasner, B. (1986). *Between give and take.* New York: Brunner/Mazel.

Boszormenyi-Nagy, I., & Spark, G.M. (1973). *Invisible loyalties.* New York: Harper & Row.

Bruch, H. (1973). *Eating disorders: Obesity, anorexia nervosa and the person within.* New York: Basic Books.

Bruch, H. (1978). *The golden cage.* London: Open Books.

Bruch, H. (1982). Anorexia nervosa: Therapy and theory. *The American Journal of Psychiatry, 139,* 1531–1538.

Bruch, H. (1985). Four decades of eating disorders. In D.M. Garner & P.E. Garfinkel (Eds.), *Handbook of psychotherapy for anorexia nervosa and bulimia* (pp. 7–18). New York: Guilford Press.

Caplan, G., & Lebovici, S. (Eds.) (1969). *Adolescence/Psychosocial perspectives.* New York: Basic Books.

Casper, R.C., Eckert, E.D., Halmi, K.A., Goldberg, S.C., & Davis, J.M. (1980). Bulimia: Its incidence and clinical importance in patients with anorexia nervosa. *Archives of General Psychiatry, 37,* 1030–1035.

de Shazer, S. (1985). *Keys to solution in brief therapy.* New York: W.W. Norton.

Feighner, J.P., Robins, E., Guze, S.B., Wooduff, R.A., Winokur, G., & Munoz, R. (1972). Diagnostic criteria for use in psychiatric research. *Archives of General Psychiatry, 26,* 57–63.

Fisch, R., Weakland, J.H., & Segal, L. (1982). *The tactics of change: Doing therapy briefly.* San Francisco: Jossey-Bass.

Garfinkel, P.E., & Garner, D.M. (1982). *Anorexia nervosa: A multidimensional perspective.* New York: Brunner/Mazel.

Garfinkel P.E., Moldofsky, H., & Garner, D.M. (1980). The heterogeneity of anorexia nervosa. *Archives of General Psychiatry, 37,* 1036–1040.

Garner, D.M., & Garfinkel, P.E. (Eds.) (1984). *Handbook of psychotherapy for anorexia nervosa and bulimia.* New York: Guilford Press.

Gilligan, C. (1982). *In a different voice: Psychological theory and women's development.* Cambridge, MA: Harvard University Press.

Gull, W.W. (1873). Anorexia nervosa (apepsia hysterical). *British Medical Journal, 2,* 527–528.

Habermas, T., & Müller, M. (1986). Das Bulimie-Syndrom: Krankheitsbild, Dynamik und Therapie. *Nervenarzt, 57,* 322–331.

Haley, J. (1963). *Strategies of psychotherapy.* New York: Grune & Stratton.

Haley, J. (1967). Toward a theory of pathological systems. In G.H. Zuk & I. Boszormenyi-Nagy (Eds.), *Family therapy and disturbed families* (pp. 11–27). Palo Alto: Science and Behavior Books.

Haley, J. (1976). *Problem-solving therapy.* San Francisco: Jossey-Bass.

Haley, J. (1985). *Conversations with Milton H. Erickson. Vol. I: Changing individuals* (p. 275). New York: Triangle Press.

Hall, A. (1987). The patient and the family. In P.J.V. Beumont, G.D. Burrows, & R.C. Casper (Eds.), *Handbook of eating disorders. Part 1: Anorexia nervosa and bulimia nervosa* (pp. 189–199). Amsterdam, New York, Oxford: Elsevier.

Hall, A., Leibrich, J., Walkey, F.H., & Welch, G. (1986). Investigation of "weight pathology" of 58 mothers of anorexia nervosa patients and 204 mothers of school girls. *Psychological Medicine, 16,* 71–76.

Hall, A., Slim, E., Hawker, F., et al. (1984). Anorexia nervosa: Long-term outcome in 50 female patients. *British Journal of Psychiatry, 145,* 407–413.

Hsu, L.K.G. (1980). Outcome of anorexia nervosa: A review of the literature (1954 to 1978). *Archives of General Psychiatry, 37,* 1041–1046.

Hsu, L.K.G. (1987). Outcome and treatment effects. In P.J.V. Beumont, G.D. Burrows, & R.C. Casper (Eds.), *Handbook of eating disorders. Part 1: Anorexia nervosa and bulimia nervosa* (pp. 371–377). Amsterdam, New York, Oxford: Elsevier.

Hsu, L.K.G., Meltzer, E.S., & Crisp, A.H. (1981). Schizophrenia and anorexia nervosa. *The Journal of Nervous and Mental Disease, 169,* 273–276.

Imber-Black, E. (1987). Idiosyncratic life cycle transitions and therapeutic rituals. In B. Carter & M. McGoldrick (Eds.), *The family life cycle: A framework for family therapy* (2nd ed.). New York: Gardner Press.

Johnson, C., & Flach, A. (1985). Family characteristics of 105 patients with bulimia. *The American Journal of Psychiatry, 142,* 1321–1324.

Karpel, M. (1976). Individuation: From fusion to dialogue. *Family Process,* 15, 65–82.

Keeney, B.P. (1983). *Aesthetics of change.* New York: Guilford Press.

Kelsey-Smith, M., & Beavers, W.R. (1981). Family assessment: Centripetal and centrifugal family systems. *The American Journal of Family Therapy, 9,* 3–12.

Lasègue, C.H. (1873). De l'anorexie hystérique. *Archives of General Medicine, 1,* 385. Translated as: On hysterical anorexia. *Medical Times and Gazette, 2,* 265–266, 367–369. Reprinted in M. Kaufman & M. Heiman (Eds.), *Evolution of a psychosomatic concept: Anorexia nervosa, a paradigm.* New York: International Universities Press, 1964.

Liebman, R., Minuchin, S., & Baker, L. (1974). An integrated treatment program for anorexia nervosa. *The American Journal of Psychiatry, 131,* 432–436.

Lorand, S., & Schneer, H.I. (Eds.) (1961). *Adolescents/Psychoanalytic approach to problems and therapy.* New York: Paul B. Hoeber.

Lowenkopf, E.L. (1983). Bulimia: Concept and therapy. *Comprehensive Psychiatry, 24,* 546–554.

MacLeod, S. (1981). The art of starvation. London: Virago Press.

Madanes, C. (1981). *Strategic family therapy.* San Francisco: Jossey-Bass.

Madanes, C. (1983). *Behind the one-way mirror: Advances in the practice of strategic therapy.* San Francisco: Jossey-Bass.

Maturana, H.R. (1978). Biology of language: The epistemology of reality. In G.A. Miller & E. Lenneberg (Eds.), *Psychology and biology of language and thought.* New York: Academic Press.

Maturana, H.R., & Varela, F.J. (1980). *Autopoesis and cognition: The realization of living.* Boston: Reidel.

Maturana, H., & Varela, F. (1987). *Der Baum der Erkenntnis.* München: Scherz.

Minuchin, S., & Fishman, H.C. (1981). *Family therapy techniques.* Cambridge, MA: Harvard University Press.

Minuchin, S., Rosman, B.L., & Baker, L. (1978). *Psychosomatic families: Anorexia nervosa in context.* Cambridge, MA: Harvard University Press.

Mitchell, J.E., Hatsukami, D., Eckert, E.D., & Pyle, R.L. (1985). Characteristics of 275 patients with bulimia. *The American Journal of Psychiatry* 142(4), 482–485.

Moley, V.A. (1983). Interactional treatment of eating disorders. *Journal of Strategic and Systemic Therapies, 2,* 10–29.

Morgan, H.G., & Russell, G.F.M. (1975). Value of family background and clinical features as predictors of long-term outcome in anorexia nervosa: Four years follow-up of 41 patients. *Psychological Medicine, 5,* 355–371.

Orbach, S. (1978). *Fat is a feminist issue.* New York: Paddington Press.

Orbach, S. (1984). Accepting the symptom: A feminist psychoanalytic treatment of anorexia nervosa. In D.M. Garner & P.E. Garfinkel (Eds.), *Handbook of psychotherapy for anorexia nervosa and bulimia.* New York: Guilford Press.

Orbach, S. (1986). *Hunger strike—The anorectic's struggle as a metaphor for our age.* New York, London: W.W. Norton.

Paul, N.L. (1987). The paradoxical nature of grief. In H. Stierlin, F.B. Simon, & G. Schmidt (Eds.), *Familiar realities* (pp. 84–98). New York: Brunner/Mazel.

Penn, P. (1982). Circular questioning. *Family Process, 21,* 267–280.

Piaget, J. (1950). *The psychology of intelligence.* New York: Harcourt, Brace.

Rosman, B.L., Minuchin, S., Baker, L., & Liebman, R. (1977). A family approach to anorexia nervosa: Study, treatment and outcome. In R.A. Vigersky (Ed.), *Anorexia nervosa* (pp. 341–348). New York: Raven Press.

Rosman, B.L., Minuchin, S., & Liebman, R. (1975). Family lunch session: An introduction to family therapy in anorexia nervosa. *American Journal of Orthopsychiatry, 45,* 846–853.

Schwartz, D.M., & Thompson, M.G. (1981). Do anorectics get well? Current research and future needs. *The American Journal of Psychiatry, 138,* 319–323.

Schwartz, R.C., Berrett, M.J., & Saba, G. (1985). Family therapy for bulimia. In D.M. Garner & P.E. Garfinkel (Eds.), *Anorexia nervosa and bulimia* (pp. 280–307). New York, London: Guilford Press.

Selvini Palazzoli, M. (1974). *Self starvation: From the intrapsychic to the transpersonal approach to anorexia nervosa.* New York: Jason Aronson.

Selvini Palazzoli, M. (1980). Why long intervals between sessions? The therapeutic control of the family-therapist suprasystem. In M. Andolfi & I. Zwerling (Eds.), *Dimensions of family therapy.* New York: Guilford Press.

Selvini Palazzoli, M. (1988). The Work of Mara Selvini Palazzoli (M. Selvini, Ed.) Northvale, NJ: Jason Aronson.

Selvini Palazzoli, M., Boscolo, L., Cecchin, G., & Prata, G. (1978). *Paradox and counterparadox.* New York: Jason Aronson.

Selvini Palazzoli, M., Boscolo, L., Cecchin, G., & Prata, G. (1980a). The problem of the referring person. *Journal of Marital and Family Therapy, 6,* 3–9.

Selvini Palazzoli, M., Boscolo, L., Cecchin, G., & Prata, G. (1980b). Hypothesizing–circularity–neutrality: Three guidelines for the conductor of the session. *Family Process, 19,* 3–12.

Simon, F.B. (1988). *Unterschiede, die Unterschiede machen.* Heidelberg, Tokyo, New York: Springer.

Simon, F.B., & Stierlin, H. (1987). Schizophrenie und Familie. *Spektrum der Wissenschaft*, May, 38–48.

Simon, F.B., Stierlin, H., & Wynne, L.C. (1985). *The language of family therapy: A systemic sourcebook.* New York: Family Process Press.

Simon, F.B., & Weber, G. (1987). Post aus der Werkstatt. *Familiendynamik, 12,* 355–362.

Sperling, E., & Massing, A. (1970). Der familiäre Hintergrund der Anorexia nervosa und die sich daraus ergebenden therapeutischen Schwierigkeiten. *Z. Psychosom. Med. Psychoanal., 16,* 130–141.

Sperling E., & Massing, A. (1972). Besonderheiten in der Behandlung der Magersuchtsfamilie. *Psyche, 25,* 357–369.

Sperling, E., Massing, A., Reich, G., Georgi, H., & Wöbbe-Mönks, E. (1982). *Die Mehrgenerationen-Familientherapie.* Göttingen: Vandenhoeck & Ruprecht.

Stierlin, H. (1977). *Psychoanalysis and family therapy.* New York: Jason Aronson.

Stierlin, H. (1978). *Delegation und Familie.* Frankfurt: Suhrkamp.

Stierlin, H. (1980). Foreword to the German edition of H. Bruch's "The Golden Cage." Frankfurt: Fischer.

Stierlin, H. (1981a). Die Beziehungsrealität Schizophrener. *Psyche, 35,* 49–65.

Stierlin, H. (1981b). *Separating parents and adolescents* (2nd enlarged edition). New York: Jason Aronson.

Stierlin, H. (1983). Family dynamics in psychotic and severe psychosomatic disorders: A comparison. *Family Systems Medicine, 1,* 41–50.

Stierlin, H. (1987). Co-individuation and co-evolution. In H. Stierlin, F.B. Simon, & G. Schmidt (Eds.), *Familiar realities* (pp. 99–108). New York: Brunner/Mazel.

Stierlin, H., Rücker-Embden, I., Wetzel, N., & Wirsching, M. (1980). *The first interview with the family.* New York: Brunner/Mazel.

Stierlin, H., Levi, L., & Savard, R. (1973). Centrifugal versus centripetal separation in adolescence: Two patterns and some of their implications. In S. Feinstein & P. Giovacchini (Eds.), *Annals of American Society of Adolescent Psychiatry, 2,* 211–239. New York: Basic Books.

Stierlin, H., & Weber, G. (1987). Anorexia nervosa: Family dynamics and family therapy. In P.J.V. Beumont, G.D. Burrows, & R.C. Casper (Eds.), *Handbook of eating disorders. Part 1: Anorexia and bulimia nervosa.* Amsterdam, New York, Oxford: Elsevier.

Theander, S. (1970). Anorexia nervosa: A psychiatric investigation of 94 female patients. *Acta Psychiatrica Scandinavica, 2/4* (Suppl.), 1–194.

Theander, S. (1983). Research on outcome and prognosis of anorexia nervosa and some results from a Swedish long-term study. *International Journal of Eating Disorders, 2,* 167–174.

Thomae, H. (1961). Anorexia nervosa (pp. 11–30). Bern: Hans Huber; Stuttgart: Ernst Klett.

Toman, W. (1976). *Family constellation: Its effects on personality and social behavior* (3rd ed.) New York: Springer.

Tomm, K. (1987). Interventive interviewing: Part II—Reflexive questioning as a means to enable self-healing. *Family Process, 26,* 167–183.

Vandereycken, W., & Pierloot, R.A. (1983). The significance of subclassification in anorexia nervosa. A comparative study of clinical features in 141 patients. *Psychological Medicine, 13* (3), 543–549.

von Foerster, H. (1970). Thoughts and notes on cognition. In P.L. Garvin (Ed.), *Cognition: A multiple view* (pp. 25–48). New York: Plenum Press.

von Foerster, H. (1984). On constructing a reality. In P. Watzlawick (Ed.), *The invented reality.* New York: W.W. Norton.

von Foerster, H. (1985). *Sicht und Einsicht.* Braunschweig: Vieweg.

von Weizsäcker, E. (1949). *Arzt und Kranker.* Stuttgart: K.F. Koehler Verlag.

von Weizsäcker, E. (1974). Erstmaligkeit und Bestätigung als Komponenten der pragmatischen Information. In V. von Weizsäcker, *Offene Systeme.* Stuttgart: Ernst Klett.

von Weizsäcker, E. (1987). Der Arzt und der Kranke/Stücke einer medizinischen Anthropologie. In *Gesammelte Schriften, Band 5.* Frankfurt: Suhrkamp.

Watzlawick, P., Beavin, J.H., & Jackson, D.D. (1967). *Pragmatics of human communication: A study of interactional patterns, pathologies and paradoxes.* New York: W.W. Norton.

Watzlawick, P., Weakland, J.H., & Fisch, R. (1974). *Change: Principles of problem formation and problem resolution.* New York: W.W. Norton.

Weber, M. (1913). Über einige Kategorien der verstehenden Soziologie. In M. Weber, *Gesammelte Aufsätze zur Wissenschaftslehre.* Tübingen: Mohr.

White, M. (1983). Anorexia nervosa: A transgenerational systems perspective. *Family Process, 22,* 255–273.

Willi, J., & Hagemann, R. (1976). Langzeitverläufe der Anorexia nervosa. *Schweiz. Med. Wschr., 106,* 1459–1465.

Wirsching, M., & Stierlin, H. (1982). *Krankheit und Familie.* Stuttgart: Klett.

Wynne, L.C., & Wynne, A.R. (1987). The quest for intimacy. In H. Stierlin, F.B. Simon, & G. Schmidt (Eds.), *Familiar realities* (pp. 60–76). New York: Brunner/Mazel.

Yager, J., Landsverk, J., & Edelstein, C.K. (1987). A 20-month follow-up study of 628 women with eating disorders. I: Course and severity. *The American Journal of Psychiatry, 144,* 1172–1177.

Ziolko, H.V. (1985). Bulimie. *Zeitschrift für Psychosomatische Medizin, 31,* 235–246.

Name Index

Subject Index

241